"This book illuminates and reminds us all of the spiritual wealth and particular contributions of Latino/a cultures and people to the broader church and community. It is a thoughtful, accessible, and moving overview. I recommend it for both Latino/a audiences and for those who need all that we bring."

—Rev. Alexia Salvatierra, Centro Latino,
Fuller Theological Seminary

"In your hands, this book may feel like a small book, but it is a very big book! It is big not because of the number of pages but rather because its brevity makes it an unexcelled basic introduction to Latina and Latino readings of Scripture. It is big because it shows the depth and the nature of our commitment to Scripture. It is big because it tells the church at large that the Bible is still relevant in our day and will be relevant wherever believers are willing to take the risk of reading it with new eyes."

—Justo L. González, immigrant, church historian,
and theologian

"*Reading the Bible Latinamente* reminds us that the only way to understand the word of God honestly and clearly is to see it through one's cultural identity and social location. In showing us ways in which Latinos and Latinas interpret the Scriptures, the authors make the case for a beautiful and transformational reading—a reading that liberates rather than discriminates, marginalizes, and oppresses people. In this way, this book is not just for the Latino/a church but for the whole of God's people."

—Al Tizon, North Park Theological Seminary

"In *Reading the Bible Latinamente*, DeBorst, Carroll, and Echevarría emphasize the unique experience of being a Latino reader of the Bible, showcasing how the Scriptures speak powerfully to the Latino community. This book captures the richness of Latino interpretation, showing that the historically marginalized readings and unique faith expressions of diverse Latino communities are not only firmly situated within *la tradición evangélica* but also invaluably contribute to it. This work truly reflects the hermeneutical realities of being a Latino Christian today, both in North America and around the world."

—**Dominick Hernández**, Talbot en Español, Talbot School of Theology, Biola University

"How does the Bible speak to the realities of Latinos/as? To read this book is to come to know the God who has asked us to love our neighbor as well as to come to know our Latino/a neighbors and to be deeply enriched. It is to come to the knowledge of righteousness or right relations for daily living in ways not previously imagined. The lives of the people portrayed are the vehicles of revelation. The topics are also ways to open discussions among those of us who are Latinos/as with the purpose of deepening and expanding our Christian traditions and practices in the diaspora."

—**Rev. Elizabeth Conde-Frazier**, independent scholar and theological educator

READING *the* BIBLE LATINAMENTE

LATINO/A INTERPRETATION FOR THE LIFE OF THE CHURCH

✳ ✳ ✳

RUTH PADILLA DEBORST, M. DANIEL CARROLL R., AND MIGUEL G. ECHEVARRÍA

Ⓑ **Baker Academic**
a division of Baker Publishing Group
Grand Rapids, Michigan

Published by Baker Academic
a division of Baker Publishing Group
Grand Rapids, Michigan
BakerAcademic.com

Library of Congress Cataloging-in-Publication Data
Names: Padilla DeBorst, Ruth, author. | Carroll R., M. Daniel, author. | Echevarría, Miguel G., Jr., author.
Title: Reading the Bible Latinamente : Latino/a interpretation for the life of the church / Ruth Padilla DeBorst, M. Daniel Carroll R., and Miguel G. Echevarría.
Description: Grand Rapids, Michigan : Baker Academic, a division of Baker Publishing Group, [2024] | Includes bibliographical references and index.
Identifiers: LCCN 2024002301 | ISBN 9781540966568 (paperback) | ISBN 9781540968272 (casebound) | ISBN 9781493447442 (ebook) | ISBN 9781493447459 (pdf)
Subjects: LCSH: Bible—Criticism, interpretation, etc.—Latin America. | Bible—Hermeneutics.
Classification: LCC BS476 .P266 2024 | DDC 220.601—dc23/eng/20240311
LC record available at https://lccn.loc.gov/2024002301

The story told at the beginning of chapter 1 is a composite.

24   25   26   27   28   29   30   7   6   5   4   3   2   1

Dedicamos este libro
a la iglesia latina en los Estados Unidos,
pueblo peregrino y esperanzado, semilla de bendición

We dedicate this book
to the Latino/a church in the United States,
a hopeful, pilgrim people, seed of blessing

CONTENTS

PREFACE

Christian Latinos and Latinas love the Bible. *Es la Palabra de Dios.* As the very Word of God, it is authoritative for our life in this country. This authority is continually reflected in how it illumines our world, offers guidance, and provides hope. That reality, however, is grounded in the deep conviction that the Scriptures *are* God's revelation to the people of God. That belief is the foundation for this book.

This statement needs some clarification. To begin with, it locates this book within our evangelical and Pentecostal traditions and churches.[1] The Latino and Latina believers in these traditions number in the millions and their churches in the tens of thousands across the denominational spectrum. This trust in the Bible can be distinct from what is held among certain sectors of Latinos and Latinas in the academy, where the Bible can be problematized as counterproductive to transformative agendas and as ideologically compromised in its very writing. While the authors of this

---

1. There are, of course, Latino/a readings within Roman Catholic circles. Note, e.g., the insightful work by Jean-Pierre Ruiz, *Reading from the Edges: The Bible and People on the Move* (Maryknoll, NY: Orbis Books, 2011).

book appreciate the work of those scholars, some of whom are personal friends, we respectfully disagree and would argue that the Old and New Testaments, as the Word of God, have amazing potential for empowering us to engage the pressing issues of identity and for challenging current ecclesial and social realities of our communities.

At least three more points are relevant for understanding the purposes behind *Reading the Bible Latinamente*. First, it is important to appreciate what this book is *not*. On the one hand, there is no attempt here to present a history of Latino/a interpretations of the Bible or to survey the various fields of academic discourse revolving around Latino/a biblical interpretation. Others within the academic guild have provided resources on matters related to those endeavors.[2]

This book also does not pretend to claim that it speaks for all Latino/a evangelicals and Pentecostals. There is no *one* reading among Latino and Latina believers that can be said to be *the* Latino/a interpretation of the Scripture. Anyone who is aware of the immense variety of Latino/a churches knows that there are all kinds of preaching, teaching, devotional and worship practices, and interpretations within the many different Baptistic, Reformed, independent, and Pentecostal (and more!) Latino/a congregations and organizations. Rather, what the authors hope to model in these pages is what an evangelical Latino/a voice that can speak to our

2. E.g., Francisco Lozada Jr. and Fernando F. Segovia, eds., *Latino/a Biblical Hermeneutics: Problematics, Objectives, Strategies*, Semeia Studies 68 (Atlanta: SBL Press, 2014); Francisco Lozada Jr., *Toward a Latino/a Biblical Interpretation*, Resources for Biblical Study 91 (Atlanta: SBL Press, 2017); Francisco Lozada Jr. and Fernando F. Segovia, eds., *Latino/a Theology and the Bible: Ethnic-Racial Reflections on Interpretation* (Lanham, MD: Lexington Books / Fortress Academic, 2021). These resources include *mujerista* (progressive Latina) voices; cf. Loida I. Martell-Otero, Zaida Maldonado Pérez, and Elizabeth Conde-Frazier, *Latina Evangélicas: A Theological Survey from the Margins* (Eugene, OR: Cascade Books, 2013), 73–89.

individual lives, families, congregations, and communities from within our faith traditions might look like.

Second, this book is not an academic tome. The authors are aware of scholarly publications on current research and debates regarding Latino/a biblical interpretation, but *Reading the Bible Latinamente* targets a wide audience. Our hope is that this little volume will prove useful to Latinos and Latinas who seek for the Bible to speak to our realities. So, we extend this offering to Latino/a pastors, laypeople, and students. Perhaps it also can be a lens for others who desire to hear and learn from a marginalized voice—that is, readers of the Bible from all ethnicities may benefit from learning about reading it *latinamente*. Footnotes have been kept to a minimum by design. We deliberately avoid jargon and technical discussions that would be topics for another kind of book.

A final item by way of introduction concerns the labels that are used for *nuestra gente*, our people. Latinos and Latinas now number sixty-four million, a fast-growing, multiracial population that now makes up almost 20 percent of the national total. Most self-identify by their personal or family country of origin in Latin America or use the terms "Hispanic" (*hispano*, *hispana*) or "Latino"/"Latina." In some academic circles and social media, "Latinx" is preferred as gender inclusive. A recent study shows that only a small percentage of Latinos and Latinas, however, use this label, and a large proportion have never heard of it.[3] Because of

3. See Luis Noé Bustamente, Lauren Mora, and Mark Hugo López, "About One-in-Four U.S. Hispanics Have Heard of Latinx, But Just 3% Use It," Pew Research Center, August 11, 2020, https://www.pewresearch.org/hispanic/2020/08/11/about-one-in-four-u-s-hispanics-have-heard-of-latinx-but-just-3-use-it/. A newer attempt to be gender inclusive is the term "Latine." An equally complex issue is the use of Spanish. See Lauren Mora and Mark Hugo López, "Latinos' Views of and Experiences with the Spanish Language," Pew Research Center, September

our commitment to our Latino/a communities and churches, we utilize "Latino" and "Latina," the combination "Latino/a," and occasionally "Hispanic."[4]

Conclusion

The three authors of this volume come from different Latino/a backgrounds. Ruth Padilla DeBorst is an Argentine American who has spent most of her life in Latin America and now splits time during the year between San José, Costa Rica, and Michigan. M. Daniel (Danny) Carroll Rodas is a Guatemalan American. He spent time in Guatemala growing up and later taught there for many years before returning to teach in the US. Miguel G. Echevarría is a Cuban American, born and raised in South Florida. All three have extensive experience in and with evangelical Latino/a churches and are involved in Latino/a theological education.

Each author has penned two chapters. Ruth probes the complexities of Latino and Latina identity in the US and then explains characteristics and commitments of a socially situated evangelical Latino/a reading of the Bible. Danny and Miguel present two chapters of readings of texts from the Old and New Testament, respectively. The expositions of these chapters also weave in the authors' backgrounds. On the one hand, this demonstrates that this book is more than an academic exercise; it represents a personal testimony of our walk with God, the Word, and the church among our people. On the other hand, these stories also exemplify

20, 2023, https://www.pewresearch.org/race-ethnicity/2023/09/20/latinos-views -of-and-experiences-with-the-spanish-language/.

4. For some, "Hispanic" is controversial because of its connection to the US Census Bureau. It appears in this volume because it is commonly used by our people; cf. M. Daniel Carroll R., *The Bible and Borders: Hearing God's Word on Immigration* (Grand Rapids: Brazos, 2020), 4–5.

the socioethnic and ecclesial diversity of our communities. What brings the authors together in this collaborative project, this effort *en conjunto* (together or in community), is our shared evangelical faith. May this volume be an encouragement for other conversations and for fresh Latino and Latina readings of Scripture that will resonate *con nuestro pueblo* (with our people).

ACKNOWLEDGMENTS

We would like to thank Anna Gissing of Baker Academic for all her encouragement and valuable input in shepherding this project to the finish line. She has been our constant champion! We also want to thank Danny's doctoral student Andrew Panaggio, a son of missionaries raised in Peru, who is a Peruvian citizen and is married to a Peruvian, for compiling the indexes. They will return to that Andean land after the completion of his studies. His also was a work of committed love for *el pueblo latino*.

CONTRIBUTORS

Ruth Padilla DeBorst is a wife of one and a mother of many, theologian, missiologist, educator, and storyteller. She has been involved in theological formation for integral mission in her native Latin America and beyond for several decades. She is the Richard Oudersluys Associate Professor of World Christianity at Western Theological Seminary and serves with the Comunidad de Estudios Teológicos Interdisciplinarios (CETI) and the International Fellowship for Mission as Transformation (INFEMIT). Along with her husband, James, she divides her year between Michigan and Costa Rica, where they are members of Casa Adobe, an intentional Christian community with deep concern for right living in relation to the whole of creation.

M. Daniel Carroll R. (Rodas) is Scripture Press Ministries Professor of Biblical Studies and Pedagogy in the graduate school of Wheaton College. Many years of involvement in Latino/a churches have led him to write extensively on the Bible and immigration, most recently *The Bible and Borders: Hearing God's Word on Immigration*. His latest books are a major commentary on the book of Amos and *The Lord Roars: Recovering the Prophetic Voice for Today*. He is coeditor with H. H. Hardy II of the forthcoming *The State of Old Testament Studies: A Survey of Recent Research*.

Miguel G. Echevarría is Associate Professor of New Testament and Greek at Southeastern Baptist Theological Seminary. He is the author of *The Future Inheritance of Land in the Pauline Epistles*, *40 Questions about the Apostle Paul*, and *Engaging the New Testament: A Short Introduction for Students and Ministers*. He has contributed commentaries on John and the Johannine epistles to *The New Testament in Color: A Multiethnic Commentary on the New Testament*. He has taught and ministered in the US and Latin America.

1

Who Are We and from Where Do We Read?

Latino/a Identity and Location

She was fifteen when the gang leader set his eyes on her and decided she would be "his girl." Her horrified father, a pastor in the neighborhood, had managed to negotiate some terms that would appease the gang without meaning the family would totally lose their precious daughter: she could return home on weekends and join the family for church. Unwilling to submit for long to this oppressive arrangement, Sofía begged her parents for a way out. On one of her weekends home, she filled her backpack with some belongings and, after receiving her parents' blessing, she embarked on the long walk north to join her aunt in Washington, DC. After a grueling trek, during which she was able to evade both narcotics traffickers and border patrol, she was held in detention for six weeks until she was released to her aunt and given a court date. A

1

fervent Christian, Sofía attends the storefront church on the one Sunday a month she is free from her very poorly paid caregiving job. She trusts that, since God has brought her safely thus far, things will work out and she will eventually get papers and make enough money to send some home. She makes time to read her Bible every night, although sometimes she is so exhausted, she falls asleep mid-sentence. She has memorized Psalm 23 and recites it for encouragement whenever she misses home or is hit by the mistreatment she receives for her poor English. She takes comfort in the biblical promises of God's care and presence among God's people.

My (Ruth's) story contrasts significantly with that of Sofía in more ways than one. While Sofía most likely has a blend of indigenous and Spanish ancestry, my DNA is even more varied. Let me explain. On the wall of the Quito Metropolitan Cathedral, in Ecuador, a plaque names Juan de Padilla among the founders of the Spanish city in 1534. One of my father's ancestors is a conquistador; but I do not say this with pride because generations of Spaniards oppressed my other ancestors, the indigenous people of those lands. At the same time, my indigenous blood is mixed with traces of Swiss-German and Scottish-Irish through my US-American mother. In other words, I am a mutt.

While Sofía traveled the perilous road of the undocumented migrant, I own many "passports of plenty." Because of my mother's place of birth, I have a US passport, which opens ever so many doors for me. Although I grew up under a US-backed dictatorship in Argentina, I received a solid public education, went on to graduate school and a PhD in the US, and have held professional jobs all my adult life. I've never had to work in a restaurant kitchen or change bedpans as Sofía does. Instead, I have a teaching job in a respected educational institution where my biculturalism is appreciated. Although my complexion is brown, since I grew up bilingual and speak English with barely a hint of foreign accent, I am white-passing and do not get discriminated against in public spaces. Because of my academic formation, I get invited to serve as the token Latina in all sorts of theological conferences in which organizers can tick the ethnicity box without needing to pay for translation. As you see, in contrast to Sofía, I have many passports of plenty!

Yet, even with all the differences between us, we are both Latina women, two of the over 62.5 million people who identified as Hispanic or Latino/a in the 2021 US census. As we seek to explore what it looks like to read the Bible *latinamente*, a necessary first question is, What or rather *who* are we as Latinos and Latinas? Clarity regarding our identity will help explain the sociocultural location from which we inevitably read Scripture. This chapter seeks to tackle those two clarifications.

Who Are We as Latinos and Latinas?

As the contrast between Sofía and me illustrates, Latinos and Latinas are, first of all, an extremely diverse people. One of my daughters teaches a predominantly Latino population in a public school in Brooklyn, where 95 percent of her students are Ecuadorean, most of them of Quechua ethnicity. One of my sons was hired to shadow Latino young people in the state of Washington but was frustrated to realize his Spanish was of little use for the Mam migrants from Guatemala. Last term my online Latino students at Western Theological Seminary came to the US from Mexico, Venezuela, Peru, El Salvador, Guatemala, and Honduras. Some were recent arrivals; some had been here for decades. Some were very conversant in English; others only understood Spanish. Some had college degrees; some did not.

We are diverse in so many ways. We are diverse in skin color: darker, lighter, and all shades in between. We are diverse in ethnic and cultural backgrounds: we are descendants of the original peoples of Latin America,[1] of slaves trafficked from the African continent, of conquistadors and colonizers from Spain and Portugal, of other blends of European, Middle Eastern, and Asian peoples. We are diverse in language use: some of us are fully immersed in *nuestro barrio* (our neighborhood), speaking only Spanish; some of us are bilingual and move fluidly between worlds; some of us do not speak Spanish. We are diverse in the forms of our Christian faith: some of our families have strong Roman Catholic backgrounds; some of us have *evangélico* faith traditions going back several generations;[2] some of us belong to historical, "conciliar" denominations and others to more independent and charismatic ones. We are diverse in life experience: some of our ancestors "were crossed by the border";[3] some of our ancestors crossed the border generations ago; some of us crossed very re-

1. A term that is increasingly used instead of "Latin America" is *Abya Yala*, since this expression focuses on the land shared by peoples from many ethnic backgrounds, a continent that is not merely Latin/European but also indigenous, African, and Asian in its makeup. The compound term was coined by the Guna (or Kuna) people who live in present-day Panama and Colombia. It means "land of plenitude and maturity" and has been employed by autochthonous groups to refer to what Europeans named America. The usage of the term is customary now in decolonial-postcolonial circles, which affirm the rights of indigenous peoples. It can be employed interchangeably with the more traditional term, "Latin America."

2. In Spanish, the term *evangélico* is not equivalent to "evangelical." Instead, it is a synonym of "Protestant," or, more specifically, it refers to "non-Catholic Christians."

3. Many years ago, my naive self was shocked when an *hermano* with a González surname in Los Angeles was unable to present in Spanish on a panel of the Fraternidad Teológica Latinoamericana. Intrigued, I inquired after his story. He explained that he could trace his Spanish ancestry and presence in California back to the mid-nineteenth century. Under Spanish and then Mexican rule, California only became a US state in 1850. For the original Spanish families settled there, what González explained to me is very true: "We never crossed the border. The border crossed us!"

cently; some of us crossed as unaccompanied minors; some of us own the passports of plenty that mean we face no borders. We are diverse in the foods we prepare and enjoy: some of us love *tacos* while others prefer *asados*; some of us eat *pupusas* while others favor *ceviche*. We are diverse in the music we savor (and maybe even dance to): bachata and merengue, tango and cumbia.

Given such diversity, we must ask, Do we have anything in common? Is there such a thing as "Latino/a culture"? Some scholars respond negatively to that query. For example, J. E. García proposes, "There is nothing that so-called Hispanics/Latinos have in common. There is no unity, no reality which stands behind the name, for there are no common properties to all Hispanics/Latinos."[4] Others, in contrast, positively highlight shared traits that justify the identification of a Latino/a people group. We share a heritage linked to the colonial expansion of Spain and, more recently, to the colonial expansion of the US in the lands south of the Rio Grande. Even though some might identify us as one *raza* (race), we are a *mezcla*, a mixture, the product of a variety of blends. Through our veins flows blood of different sources, of both conquerors and conquered people. First, we are not simply of Latin European extract; instead, we are *mestizo*—blended with the blood of the original inhabitants of the land—and we are *mulato*, blended with the blood of black Africans. We sit squarely, though not necessarily comfortably, in the liminal space between several people groups.[5] Added to that original *mestizaje* is the more recent and ongoing blend that continues to take place within the US itself through intermarriage and cultural adaptations, and the

4. Jorge E. García, quoted in Daniel A. Rodríguez, *A Future for the Latino Church: Models for Multilingual, Multigenerational Hispanic Congregations* (Downers Grove, IL: IVP Academic, 2011), 26.

5. The term "liminal" derives from the Latin *limen*, which means "threshold" and points to "in-betweenness."

consequent contrasting experiences of "native born" and "foreign born" Latinos in this country. A third-generation Mexican-American scholar explains: "While we often feel rejected by the foreign-born for being *agringado* (Americanized), we also perceive that we are treated as second-class citizens in the country of our birth and often treated as 'outsiders' in the churches of the dominant group."[6] Ours is the hyphenated experience of constant identity negotiation. We are Salvadoran-American, Ecuadorean-American, Nuyorican, US-born Latinos and Latinas, and so on. This, however, does not make us less a people: it simply makes us "both-and" people who, together, inhabit an "in-between" place.

In addition to our mixed heritage, and in many ways because of it, we also often share a condition of marginality in the dominant culture of the US. This exclusion is clearly painful. And it is particularly crippling when it gets institutionalized in policies and restrictions to our basic human rights. We can struggle with exile, with family separation and detentions, with racism and discrimination, with insufficient health care and limited educational opportunities, with sub-employment, unjust labor practices, and other forms of oppression. But *la lucha* (this complex and complicated set of struggles) has also built our character through the decades and across the miles. We have developed resilience and an amazing capacity to adapt and even to thrive. Many of us are bicultural and bilingual, gifts that make us ideal mediators and negotiators. Our families tend to be a source of strength for us when they are cohesive, extended, and intergenerationally rich, with *abuelos* and *abuelas* contributing *dichos* (sayings) from their stores of wisdom, medicinal cures for many maladies, and storied *recuerdos* (memories) from other times and other lands.

6. Rodríguez, *Future for the Latino Church*, 35.

following poem was written by a young MDiv student at Western Theological Seminary for a class on Christian Life and Mission. Christy Escobar was born in the Southside of Chicago. Her Salvadoran father migrated north in 1984, during the civil war in his native country. Her maternal grandmother is from Guanajuato, Mexico; her maternal grandfather, from Cerritos, San Luis Potosí, Mexico, migrated at age nineteen and worked as a bracero in Texas.[7] Christy's poem illustrates and evokes the strengths of our *pueblo* that allow us to thrive in spite of all the challenges many of us confront.

Small Things, Big Love by Christy Escobar[8]

When I think of enough, I think of a Ritz cracker.
Bite-down, crunchy sound, about three-quarters of the
   cracker, is delicious.

The other quarter takes to dust.
Sitting in the corners of your mouth
      down your shirt,
         floating to the floor
This cracker, a labor of love
a gift to us
Boxes and boxes and boxes, my sister and I cannot see
   over them.

They take up our garage.
They take up our kitchen.
They take up a small corner under my bed for secret
   safekeeping.
They will last us a year.

---

7. "Braceros" were Mexican agricultural workers hired by the US as part of a special program meant to cover the labor gap created during World War II. This program lasted until 1964. The term derives from the Spanish word *brazos* (arms) because these men were manual laborers.

8. Included with express permission from the author, Christy Escobar.

Small things, big love.

Snacks were a privilege, a treat, and this Ritz cracker was
  magic.

Hungry? Eat some Ritz.
Feeling munchy? Eat some Ritz.
Late night, midnight snack? Ritz.
Friends coming over? Bust out some damn Ritz.

Year 8, I was a walking, talking, beaming commercial for
  Ritz crackers.
Even the hamster could clean up the crumbs.

Small things, big love.

The year of the Ritz cracker was holy.
The giver our Elisha, the crackers, our oil jugs

We didn't have much, but we had Ritz
Our. Cup. Over. Flows . . .

Small things, big love.

I wake up, and I count.

I hear the thank yous in my ma's voice:

"There is so much to be grateful for," she says
"We have more than so many others," she says

I often wondered, *why is she here?*
Why doesn't she work?

She tells me "We're gonna be broke either way, may as well
  be broke on our own terms."
Her resistance,
her own systems,
her terms gave us small things, big love.

My Pa—served the economy but not their army.
So this country gave him small things.

But oh, he gave us big love.
A rare dinner without him, a rare Saturday without play.

Singing in the kitchen to his "honey bun."
Tucking us in with a mint-toothpaste-scented prayer.

His resistance, his persistence, his rebellion . . .
It gave us small things, big love.

He describes his country in three words:
Big, free, and growing.

"You see this flower?" he says
"In my country, they grow big and free."

"You see that river?" he asks
"At home, there is a river who runs big and free."

"Do you want to move home?" I ask
"Would you all come with me?" he asks back.

For him, this country has small things, but we are his
    big love.

So we pay his land tribute.
We turn Salvadorian seeds to Midwestern gardens.

We swim in rivers to honor Mother Lempa.
We bow to the south, where she keeps life turning.

We thank her for giving us our father
And pupusas . . .
And chicharrones . . .

Small things, big love.

We lay hands on one another when home feels far,
singing to each other home remedies.

Sana colita de rana si no sana hoy sanará mañana
With gratitude, we become one another's home.

And we find enough in our laughter
And we find enough in our *besos y abrazos*

And we find God in our *bendiciones*
And Christ in our *comunidad*
And the spirit in our guts and our hearts
And one stitch at a time, we bind up and close up these
  wounds to weave together . . . a straw hat?

Hat? Why a hat?
Because of course! Small things, big love.

We owe this hat for keeping my 'buelo from frying in the
  Mexican sun
And for giving my other 'buelo a shield to work in
  Salvadorian soil

And we will tip it in peace and in *Felicidades*
To those who thought that they needed more to get enough

But look, we got this hat from our friend Just Enough
  when you thought you needed More Enough

And Just Enough, she is curious. She wants to ask—Don't
  you want small things that give you big love?

Just enough oil in just enough jugs . . .
Allow us to give you this good news

Allow us to be your Elisha
And we can sing to one another home remedies.

Small remedies for big wounds to make sure we don't rush
To make sure we laugh and eat and toast to the good stuff
To make sure we stop and turn the soil in its season
And stop to pick the fruit when it's ripe

To make sure the food is spiced just right.

And like salted to perfection,
Like a good long nap
Like the right-sized straw hat
And dare I say it—like a Ritz cracker
Together we might find small things, big love.

We may not all enjoy Ritz crackers or share in many of the experiences Christy portrays, but extended family, memories or dreams of home, songs, home remedies, food, a yearning for full life in the "in-between" are gifts of our *pueblo*, and they constitute the fertile soil out of which those of us who identify as Christian Latinos and Latinas approach Scripture.

From Where Do We Read the Bible?

The second question this chapter addresses is this: From where do we read the Bible as Latinas and Latinos? Behind this question is the conviction that there is no such thing as a neutral, de-culturized, or de-contextualized point of departure as we engage with the biblical story. We might have been led to believe that historical theological articulations inherited from Europe and this country are pure and objective. But in reality, as Ecuadorean René Padilla explains, "The process of arriving at the meaning of Scripture is significantly conditioned not only by who we are as individuals but also by several social forces, the patterns and ideals of our particular culture, and our particular historical situation."[9] This multifaceted location inevitably marks what we see or hear and to what we remain unaware of or indifferent to.

9. C. René Padilla, *La Palabra interpretada: Reflexiones sobre hermenéutica contextual* (Lima: AGEUP, 1989), 3. English translation by Ruth Padilla DeBorst.

In his now classic *Santa Biblia: The Bible through Hispanic Eyes*, historian Justo González portrays the place from which Latinos approach Scripture: "What we mean by 'Hispanic eyes' is the perspective of those who claim their Hispanic identity as part of their hermeneutical baggage and also read the Scripture within the context of a commitment to the Latino struggle to become all that God wants us and all of the world to be—in other words, the struggle for salvation/liberation."[10] Hispanic identity, a certain approach to Scripture, a commitment to a people, and a passionate engagement in its struggle: these are all components that, woven together, constitute the place from which we read the Bible. Let's explore them together.

We Read from Our Hispanic Identity

The first part of this chapter fleshed out what we mean by Hispanic or Latino/a identity. In essence, ours is a *mestizo*, hybrid nature. We are "in-betweeners." And it is from that ethnic, social, and political location that we read Scripture. We naturally, then, connect with the biblical stories of other people who live on the move, between places and cultures, people who are constantly negotiating value, belonging, and acceptance of our contribution. We identify with Abraham and Sarah, migrating to unknown lands. We recognize ourselves in Naomi and her family forced to migrate for lack of food and in Ruth as she plans out survival strategies. We know what it is like to flee violence to a strange place, like Mary and Joseph with baby Jesus. We see ourselves in the early Christians in diaspora around the empire of the day. Chapters 3 through 6 delve deeply into these connections, so we need not detail them further here.

10. Justo González, *Santa Biblia: The Bible through Hispanic Eyes* (Nashville: Abingdon, 1996), 29.

We Read from a Believing Trust in Scripture as God's Word

My grandfather Carlos was not an extremely learned man. I'm not even sure he finished grade school. But could he ever recite Scripture! He cited long passages from the Reina y Valera 1909 version without stumbling once. He insisted that my father and his siblings learn Bible verses by heart. And he referred to them in normal, everyday conversations with the family—and even with strangers. The Bible was his friend!

A hymn I recall from my growing-up years in Buenos Aires reflects this trusting relationship between Latino/a believers and the Bible:

> Santa Biblia, para mí eres un Tesoro aquí.
> Tu contienes con verdad la divina voluntad.
> Tu me dices lo que soy, de quién vine y a quién voy.[11]

The entire hymn, which is enthusiastically sung in churches of many different denominations, expresses deep trust that the Bible is a source of insight and strength for life and not merely a doctrinal compendium or a set of ethical prescriptions. The Bible is God's Word for God's people, and we breathe it, memorize it, recite it, and quote it in our daily interactions. In González's words, "We are not speaking of the biblical text as if it were dead letter, ancient history, distant memories. We are speaking of a text in which we find ourselves, our very lives."[12] Referring to a study of how marginalized Latino/a Pentecostal communities read the Bible, Esa Autero explains, "The textual horizon and the present-day situation

11. This is the Spanish version of a hymn originally written in English in the early nineteenth century by John Burton, translated and adapted by Pedro Castro. "Holy Bible, book divine, precious treasure, thou art mine; mine to tell me whence I came, mine to teach me what I am."
12. González, *Santa Biblia*, 18.

13

merged and the boundary between the biblical story and the story of the readers became blurred."[13] We see ourselves in the stories of the Bible; we identify with the characters, their strengths and weaknesses; we fall and rise with the plot of their lives.

González qualifies this approach as precritical or premodern,[14] Padilla terms it "intuitive,"[15] and erudite scholars might dismiss it as naive. The assumption in this approach is that the Bible is accessible to simple people and not exclusively to theologians. Our *abuelos* and *abuelas* might not have finished grade school, but many of them can recite long biblical passages by heart, and they cite them opportunely in crucially needed times. The biblical text is part of their wisdom repository. As Latino communities, we engage in a life-giving conversation with the passages of the Bible. The Bible speaks to us because we believe it and tend not to complicate matters with critical questioning about the validity of the claims it contains. We believe the Holy Spirit gifts us with the capacity to enter the story the Bible tells. Further, "we read the Bible, not primarily to find out what we are to do, but to find out who we are and who we are to be. The Bible is good to us in that it answers those questions with a word of hope and affirmation."[16] What we seek as we read the Bible is not simply intellectual understanding or abstract truths. We seek—and find—nourishment for the everyday life of our community.

We Read from within the Believing Community, the Church

Overall, as a believing community, we read the Bible from our kitchen table far more commonly than from an office desk. Al-

13. Esa Autero, "Reading the Epistle of James with Socioeconomically Marginalized Immigrants in the Southern United States," *Pneuma* 39 (2017): 529.

14. González, *Santa Biblia*, 117.

15. Padilla, *La Palabra Interpretada*, 6.

16. González, *Santa Biblia*, 115.

though some theologians have sprung from among us who read, write, and publish with sophisticated terminology, most of us perceive ourselves as belonging to a broad, extended church family who speaks the daily faith language of our people. We are *hermanos* and *hermanas* (siblings) who seek to *crecer en la fe* (grow in faith) in order to *pelear la buena batalla* (fight the good fight) and *dar un buen testimonio* (be faithful witnesses). As further portrayed in chapter 2, we read *en conjunto* (communally). The fervor of our frequent and celebratory church gatherings as a church community are rooted in Scripture, and this propels us forward, even when the going gets rough, when our families are separated by legalities, when we are denied access to certain jobs because we lack certain documentation, when we are looked down on and face very limited opportunities because of the color of our skin. Together, we navigate the turbulent waters.

We Read from within **la Lucha** *(the Struggle)*

Although many Latinos and Latinas have broken paths forward within the dominant US-American society and achieved certain levels of recognition in academia, business, and the political scene, the great majority is still marginalized, stigmatized, and discriminated against. Stereotypes about Latina and Latino people abound and are often reinforced by popular media. Latino men are often portrayed as dangerous and violent, while Latina women are depicted as over-sexualized temptresses. "Lazy," "dirty," "job-stealers," "criminals," "illegals"—these are all labels commonly attached to Hispanics. The composite of these images leads to us being seen as "always other," as the "eternal outsiders." Further, and beyond the personal challenges posed by these stereotypes, structures and systems are perpetuated that exclude us and limit our ability to live full lives. We face limitations in terms of access to health care, education, and employment. Although we have not been officially bought and sold as slaves, our working conditions are often subhuman. We suffer maltreatment in the criminal system. We suffer racism: our brown, black, and *mulato* bodies are victims of hate crimes.

Ours is the constant struggle for survival in inhospitable environments, the struggle to be known, appreciated, and accepted, to be granted opportunities alongside people of other ethnicities and skin colors in a nation that has illusorily been cast as a welcoming refuge for the tired, the poor, and the huddled masses in need of a home.[17] We experience the mismatch between the American dream and our less-than-dreamlike condition.

And it is precisely from within the deep discomfort of that mismatch, from within the struggle for survival, that we read the Bible. The struggle itself grants us vistas that are usually veiled to people who live comfortable lives. As we read the Bible from our particular location, we cannot but encounter the God who hears the cries of the downtrodden, like the Israelites in Egypt, and opens a way through the sea to liberate them. Consequently, we believe God can intervene today in the midst of our limitations to help us overcome them. We cannot but hear the voice of the prophets who in the name of God denounce injustice and oppression. Consequently, we are moved to denounce wrongdoing against our people today. We see Jesus not only teaching but also freeing, healing, and saving. Consequently, we believe we can be freed, healed, and saved today. We cannot but witness the efforts of the early church to make sure no one among them had need. Consequently, we accompany one another in our *comunidad* (community), even if only with Ritz crackers. And we say yes to

17. Words from Emma Lazarus's 1883 poem, mounted on the pedestal of the Statue of Liberty.

the story the Bible tells! Yes! No matter how others view us, we are confident that we too are created in the image of the triune God. We too are fully human, even when we are told otherwise. We too can transcend suffering and carve out space to thrive as individuals, as families, as communities. We are confident that we too—Latinos and Latinas—will one day be part of the great multitude from every nation, tribe, people, and language who will stand in worship before the throne of God (Rev. 7:9). Consequently, we can join in heartfelt worship today while also standing tall and continuing to break ways forward even in an inhospitable land.

In sum, then, we read from our Hispanic identity, from a believing approach to Scripture as God's Word, and from a commitment to our suffering people and a passionate engagement in its struggle. This outlook is a true gift! We see things others do not as we engage with Scripture, and we have insights to share with the rest of the church if it has ears to hear.

2

Reading Latinamente

How Do We Read the Bible?

I was ever so happy to be in Quito, Ecuador, with my grandmother! I had recently received my fifteenth birthday special gift from my parents. No big *quinceañera* (the traditional Latino/a celebration when a girl turns fifteen) in my family. Instead, we could choose a significant, larger-than-usual gift: a typewriter, a camera, or a cassette-tape recorder. I had very determinedly chosen the latter and carried it with me proudly from Argentina to Ecuador. Now was my chance: I could interview *Mamita*, as we endearingly called our paternal grandmother, and record her life story for posterity. I imagined sitting next to her on the couch and listening silently and intently for long hours. But that was not to be.

"*M'ijita*," she began, "*vamos a la cocina*" (Let's go to the kitchen).

It was there, amid the sounds and scents of onion chopping and plantains frying, that I heard about the nuns and the delicate lace embroidering of her tiny fingers as a child in the convent school. About her excitement as she joined her father in Eloy Alfaro's revolution against the conservative Ecuadorean government of the day. About being married off against her will, and far too young, to an older military man from whom she had, happily, been widowed. About *Papito* (Grandpa) Carlos, his search for work in Colombia, and how she had packed up all their belongings and all the kids and followed him as he tailored suits for wealthy people in one town after another before settling in Los Cuadros, Bogotá. About their return to Ecuador and the eventual departure of her sons for studies in the US and their marriage to women in *el Norte*.

The only time she put down her knife and paused in her cooking was when she began telling me how she and *Papito* had finally given in to *tío* (uncle) Heriberto's entreaties and joined the *Alianza* church (Christian Missionary Alliance) in Quito. Tears ran down her wrinkly face as she joyfully shared how their newfound faith had brought light and freedom into their lives. "You see," she explained, "we finally encountered God's Word! I had never read the Bible! But we discovered it truly is a lamp unto our feet and a light unto our way! Come, come, the food can wait," she said, leading me by the hand to the table. "Let me tell you what a difference the Bible made in our lives!"

Now, my grandmother had not finished grade school. She actually struggled even to read. But there was not a single meal that was not topped off by *Papito* reading a Bible passage and the two of them discussing it before spending a long time in prayer. Rather than an erudite, scholarly approach to the text, theirs was a life-imbued conversation with the story brought to life in the reading. When it was not under *Papito*'s arm on the way to church, the old, tattered, black-covered book lay as the centerpiece of their humble table and was open at every single meal as well as at many times in between.

This chapter seeks to portray how many Latinas and Latinos approach Scripture, responding to the question "*How* do we read?" I propose three main markers, all illustrated by the story of *Mamita* and *Papito*: (1) We read *sencillamente* (straightforwardly), with a simple, trusting faith in the Bible as the Word of God; (2) we read together, in community, *en conjunto*; and (3) we read *en el camino*, along the way of daily life, with the scents and flavors of *lo cotidiano* (everyday life).

We Read *Sencillamente*

Like *Mamita* and *Papito*, our people tend to approach the Bible *sencillamente*, unassumingly, straightforwardly, with a simple, trusting faith that it is the Word of God for the people of God. Certainly, my grandparents were proud of all their children, who, though from a very humble background, had excelled in their studies. All four sons had achieved PhDs in the US or the UK, two of them in theology. I doubt, however, that either my theologian dad or my theologian uncle knew more portions of Scripture by heart than did my grandparents. Many an evening was spent with *Papito* and his brother Heriberto reciting entire books of the Bible as we kids nodded off. For them, the passages were not dead letters to be scrutinized and dissected but rather words given by God to nourish them as God's people, to sustain their faith, to encourage them when the going got tough, to convict them of sin, to call them to repentance, and to assure them of forgiveness. They had no need to question the text or to uncover original sources, debate authorship, or doubt authorial intent. They simply received the Bible as God's Word and as a gift that shed light on their way.

Their Bible reading was marked by trust and bathed in prayer: a brief prayer before the reading and a long, detailed prayer after the reading. I remember being astounded at how my grandparents persevered daily in praying for one of their daughters who had disappeared years before. I thought them naive and overly trusting. But after long years of absence, my aunt finally reconnected with the family and proved me wrong! Their confidence that God speaks through the Word nourished my grandparents' confidence that God *is* at work in the world and that, consequently, they could bring all of life's daily struggles and concerns to God in trusting prayer. God's Word inspired hope and shed light on their lives.

Of course, not all Latinos/as in this country are as poor and uneducated as were my grandparents. Many among us have the privilege of studying Hebrew, Greek, biblical sciences, and hermeneutics. Many of us are acquiring valuable tools that enable us to parse out themes and subthemes, to translate and interpret the ancient texts that compose the canon. These skills allow us to teach and preach, to encourage and nurture the church. Obviously, in order for our scholarship to truly contribute to holistic Christian life and witness in the world, we need to remain close to faith communities on the ground, to local churches, reading *with* our *hermanos* and *hermanas en la fe* (siblings in the faith) and *for* our people in ways that are sensitive and meaningful to the familial, social, cultural, and political dimensions of their lives. This rooted engagement allows for a fruitful dialogue between more scholarly and more intuitive readings of Scripture. As Latinos and Latinas, we have the opportunity to offer the riches of our people's reading to the broader church and to the academic community. At the same time, the hope is that even those of us with access to theological education will never lose the simple, trusting, prayerful faith that keeps us open to God's voice through the story the Bible tells so that we might believingly read ourselves into that story and allow the Spirit to continue telling it through our lives as we encounter all its sorrows and joys!

We Read Together, in Community, *en Conjunto*

As a linguist, I have always been struck by how certain languages develop terms that are unavailable in other languages. I remember my astonishment back in college when I learned that people in the UK have dozens of words for rain! Language and thought move in reciprocal relationship to each other and both reveal and reinforce cultural values and relationships. Aquiles Martínez puts it this way: "Through language, we interpret and conceptualize the world around us, communicate with one another and establish relationships, create community, and change and preserve our values and ideas."[1] It is not surprising, then, that in a culture as highly relational as the Latino/a one, we have terms that do not even exist in more individualistic ones. For example, how do non-Latinos express the relationship that exists between the mother of the bride and the mother of the groom? There is no term! In Spanish we use the term *consuegra* (co-mother-in-law). Likewise, we have the words *concuñados* (co-brothers-in-law), *concuñadas* (co-sisters-in-law), and even *comadres* (co-mothers or co-godmothers) and *compadres* (co-fathers or co-godfathers). The existence of these terms reveals how important familial and communal relationships are in our culture. We live, grow, fight, reconcile, and continue forward in community. And in community we read and glean meaning from Scripture.

1. Aquiles Ernesto Martínez, "U.S. Hispanic/Latino Biblical Interpretation: A Critique from Within," *Theology Today* 68, no. 2 (2011): 134–48, here 145.

Additionally, in Spanish there is a linguistic distinction between the singular and the plural second person. While in English the term "you" can refer either to an individual or to a group, in Latin American and US-Hispanic Spanish, *tú*, *vos*, and *usted* are used to address one person and *ustedes* is used to address more than one person. In an individualistic culture, biblical injunctions to "you" tend to be read as pertaining to a single person, and the collective reference can easily be lost. For example, 1 Corinthians 3:16 in English reads, "Do you not know that you are God's temple and that God's Spirit dwells in you?" (RSV). Does this "you" refer to an individual Christian or to the church as a whole? It is ambiguous but tends to be read in English as referring to a single person. Meanwhile, the same text is rendered in Spanish as: "*¿No saben que* ustedes *son templo de Dios y que el Espíritu de Dios habita en* ustedes?" (NVI). In this case, the temple of God is a metaphor clearly attributed to the collective body of the church and not to any one individual. There is one temple composed of many members ("you" plural).

Again, language and culture are mutually reinforcing phenomena. Given that our Latino/a cultural matrix is strongly collectivist, it follows naturally that our default approach to the biblical text is a communal one. We read in plural. This does not mean simply that we tend to read the Bible together, in our *cultos* (worship services) even more than in times of private devotion. This does not only refer to the family Bible reading around the table of my *abuelos* along with every meal. It means that we tend to read not merely as individuals for the sake of our personal nourishment but as members of a collective body with that plurality in mind and heart. We interpret from within and for the sake of our faith community.

This communal lens, our reading *en conjunto*, grants us vistas less accessible to people from dominantly individualistic cultures.

We are especially keyed into both the strengths and the joys as well as the conflicts and the downfalls of a people, like the Israelites in the desert or the community of first followers of "The Way" as portrayed in Acts and the letters of the New Testament. We see ourselves reflected in some of the challenges of an Old Testament community making its way across the desert into the promised land. We identify with a New Testament community struggling to bridge difference, find common ground, and live justly as an intercultural body.[2] Also, like the Jewish and gentile Christian followers of Jesus, we are not always *un pequeño pueblo muy feliz* (one small, very happy people);[3] we have our fair share of conflicts and misunderstandings, drawn together as we are from many disparate points of origin and traditions (Mexican, Puerto Rican, Cuban, Central American, and so on).

At the same time, we do know what it looks like to rally together, setting our particularities aside and supporting one another as *hermanas* and *hermanos* when we stand in need of support or are marginalized by the dominant culture. Just as we share Salvadoran *pupusas*, Venezuelan *arepas*, Ecuadorean *ceviches*, Colombian *ajiacos*, and Mexican *moles* in a church potluck, we exchange expertise for navigating the vagaries of immigration policies and job opportunities. And it is out of this *hermandad* (siblinghood) that we engage with Scripture and seek, together, to discern God's Word for us and what our calling is as God's people in God's world. We gather very often in small group Bible studies and discipleship

2. An "intercultural" community is not merely "multicultural." While a multicultural group is composed of people of diverse cultural identities and backgrounds, in an intercultural one members step out beyond their differences and engage so meaningfully with others that they are personally changed.

3. Reference to a well-known *corito* (chorus) among Latinos titled "Somos un pequeño pueblo muy feliz" (We are a small, very happy community), written by Arnaldo Christianini.

groups centered on Scripture, and we seek to apply the teaching to our lives as faith communities. We do not simply ask, "What does this passage say to my life?" but instead, "What lessons do we derive together from this passage that inform the way we live as a body of believers?"

So, as did many of our *abuelos* and *abuelas*, we read in community, *en conjunto*, with a trusting faith that, through the Bible, God talks to us in the thick of life.[4] And this leads us to the third characteristic of our approach to Scripture.

We Read *en el Camino,* along the Way of Daily Life

Daily life for many Latinos and Latinas in this country is not quite what it was billed to be. The American dream that enticed so many families across borders has proven rather elusive. Certainly, many of us have left behind intense violence, including threats to our lives, deprivation, and poverty. But having fled from one real or figurative hot spot has not always guaranteed safe haven or abundant provision. Many of us fled one hot spot and landed in another! Most of us work long hours, often in more than one job, and our pay is low. Our neighborhoods are often less than secure, and our kids' schools are threatened by gun violence. We are often considered suspect and are held back in jobs and education simply because of our origin or the color of our skin. Most of us who pastor and lead churches are bivocational, meaning

4. Worth noting is that the production of this volume is also an example of working *en conjunto*. The authors come from different Latino backgrounds: Cuban, Guatemalan, and Colombo-Argentine. We bring very diverse life experiences, and we represent a variety of fields of study. Yet the book in your hands is not a mere compilation of individual contributions but, instead, the product of the mutual exchange and feedback among three Latino/a theologian practitioners working together to offer a cohesive whole.

that we have our regular breadwinning jobs and then offer time to our congregations after hours, usually sacrificing family time and rest. Our lives are not easy. We bear the burden of injustice and yearn for relief.

At the same time, we know that God cares for us! We hold together as families and communities, resiliently breaking ways forward together and frequently sending money back to family members in the south. And we do know how to celebrate! We celebrate family birthdays, *quinceañeras*, anniversaries, and national holidays with traditional food, music, and togetherness. We celebrate as faith communities with festive church potlucks and all-night *vigilias* (praise and prayer gatherings).

Our daily lives as a community are marked by both struggle and celebration. And it is this mixed experience that we bring into conversation with the Bible. Like *Mamita*, citing Scripture as she dipped the *plátanos* (plantains) in the batter before frying them in her tiny kitchen. Like *Papito*, reciting Bible texts to his grandchildren as he laid out and cut the cloth for the next suit on the kitchen table, the only one in their simple house.

Most of us do not have the luxury of withdrawing from the daily grind so as to spend long hours in extensive exploration of the biblical text with the aid of primary sources and erudite commentaries in order to articulate scholarly explanations and derive from them elaborate implications. Most of us approach Scripture along the way of life, from within our everyday experience, from *lo cotidiano*. We believe God talks to us today through the Word and the Spirit in the midst of our occupations and preoccupations, in the midst of *la lucha* for survival and belonging. We trust that God sees us when we are in the factory during the night shift, cleaning *la señora*'s bathroom, working extra to make rent this month. We cling to the certitude that, because of God's grace in

Christ and thanks to the work of the Spirit, God meets us in the daily toil, and even the most menial occupation can become an expression of worship to God.

Again, some of us have "made it" in this land. We no longer live on the precarious edge but instead hold relatively secure jobs, have the privilege of guaranteed income, and can even visit our families across the country or in the Caribbean, Central America, or South America without breaking our bank account. We are granted the luxury of distance from the daily grind in order to study and research, to reflect and write. The challenge for us is to remain engaged with our *pueblo* so that we might feel their struggles, be moved by their daily realities, and join forces with God's liberating Spirit to seek justice and affirm the dignity of all—be they longtime residents or newcomers to this country.

Conclusion

We, Latinos and Latinas, are a *pueblo* diverse and variegated, yet who share many common experiences. For some of us, historic political and territorial shifts have made us strangers in a land that once belonged to our ancestors; for some, the shifts are more recent and have forced us to migrate from other lands to this one. One way or another, we are all members of a diaspora, living in a certain exile, swimming in social and cultural in-between waters, which we navigate in different ways as part of our daily struggle for survival, belonging, and acceptance as worthy members of the broader community and, as Christians, of the *familia de la fe* (the family of faith). It is from that location, our Hispanic identity and our daily struggle, *lo cotidiano*, that we read the Bible *sencillamente, en conjunto*, with a believing trust in the Bible as the Word of God and as a light unto our way. As we so read—boldly out of our identity and not in spite of it—and we so witness to the transformational power of God's Word, we contribute to the church and society at large.[5] More than some new or particular exegetical method, what we offer our people and the broader community of Jesus followers are these core commitments that spell out our way of approaching the biblical text.

When we read ourselves into the story of God's good work, portrayed from Genesis to Revelation and being told even today through God's people, we recognize ourselves in the biblical characters and learn alongside them. What encouragement can we gain from God's presence and provision for the migrant people of Israel as retold in the Old Testament? How does God's choice to covenant with that *pueblo* so that they might be a blessing to others mark our vocation as a diaspora *pueblo*? What lessons might we glean from the joys and struggles of the *comunidad* of early followers of Jesus to come together across ethnic and cultural barriers? The following four chapters dig into questions like these. They lay out vistas that we are gratefully granted as *pueblo* Latino and that can—by God's grace—become gifts offered to all who are willing to acknowledge and receive them.

5. About people like us, Fenggang Yang and Helen Rose Ebaugh say, "Rather than immigrants 'de-Christianizing' religion in America, they have, in fact, 'de-Europeanized' American Christianity." "Transformations in New Immigrant Religions and Their Global Implications," *American Sociological Review* 66, no. 2 (2001): 269–88, here 271.

3

Strangers in a Strange Land

Old Testament I

Stories. Stories fascinate us. Not only stories that we might read in books or see in movies or on TV but our own personal stories. Stories about where we came from, stories about family and, as Latinos and Latinas, about roots in another place. Those stories are different from the stories that define this country and the spaces in which we move—school, the playground, the mall, and work. Our experiences here are marked profoundly by our heritage from south of the border, and that impacts how we talk and feel, how we do birthdays and Christmas, why we celebrate *quinceañeras*, what we eat, and the music we listen to. These are stories that are the foundations of our identity, our *latinidad* in this largely Anglo culture.

There is variety in our narratives. To begin with, countries of origin are not the same. Some trace connections back to Mexico, others to Guatemala, Cuba, Puerto Rico, Argentina, and more. For many of us, Spanish is the language of home and our *barrio*, *el supermercado* (the supermarket), and church—even if we speak with assorted accents and *modismos* (idioms). Others speak something akin to what is called *Spanglish*, while others do not speak Spanish at all.[1] Comfort foods differ, and we cheer for our own favorite *fútbol* (soccer) club in our countries of origin and national teams. Some of us are brown, some white, some black, and some a combination of these. Some have an indigenous background; others are of African, more European, or even Asian stock. This amazing mix gives our cultures incredible richness.[2]

This variety is infinite. Yet with all of this, as Latinas and Latinos we share broad cultural bonds and, most importantly, a common story of migration, whether as immigrants ourselves or as first-, second-, or third-generation children of those who came before us. Our stories are part of a larger one of over two centuries of migration into the US. The sacrifices of our parents or *abuelos* and *abuelas*, laced with both disappointments and small victories, and our sense of being "perpetual foreigners" unite us. So, when we come together, even if we are from diverse national, racial, and ethnic backgrounds, we give each other a hug, laugh,

1. For a quick snapshot of language use, see "For Latinos, English Proficiency Has Increased and Spanish Use at Home Has Decreased," Pew Research Center, September 9, 2021, https://www.pewresearch.org/ft_2021-09-09_keyfactslatinos _08/. Proficiency in Spanish and English is often a reflection of whether the person is first-, second-, or third-generation Latino/a.

2. The term many employ to describe these mixtures is *mestizaje*, although it is disputed. Some prefer to speak about *hibridez* (hybridity). See Néstor Medina, *Mestizaje: (Re)Mapping Race, Culture, and Faith in Latina/o Catholicism* (Maryknoll, NY: Orbis Books, 2009); Daniel Orlando Álvarez, *Latin@ Identity and Pneumatological Perspective: Mestizaje and Hibridez* (Cleveland: Centre for Pentecostal Theology, 2016).

and share a meal because of something deep inside that somehow, at some level, connects us.

Our shared faith also brings us *chilangos, chapines, boricuas, porteños, ticos,* and *nicas* (the list goes on!) together.[3] We gather in Spanish-speaking or bilingual churches, or in Anglo or multi-ethnic churches, and even there our unique larger story resonates among us in diverse ways.

What many of us do not realize is that our migrant stories find echoes in Scripture. The Old Testament is full of accounts of people who had to move for all sorts of reasons—violence, hunger, forced deportation, and family feuding—and live in other contexts. We find in its pages people just like us, who migrate and wrestle with life in a different country.[4] The Word of God is truly a powerful word for us, *now* and *here.*

When we read the Old Testament, it is natural to seek general principles for life. This is a good and essential exercise, but as Latinos and Latinas we can miss that its stories mirror our own; they become *our* stories. They can help us understand who we are and how God is with us in our journeys as strangers in a strange land. Of the many from which I (Danny) could choose, I have picked four stories that everyone might know: Abram's move to Canaan, Joseph in Egypt, Daniel in Babylon, and Ruth in Bethlehem.[5] These stories can surprise us.

3. These are nicknames for people from Mexico City, Guatemala, Puerto Rico, Buenos Aires, Costa Rica, and Nicaragua, respectively. Nicknames abound in Latin America!

4. In what follows, I focus on those who have come to the US. Because of political conflict and violence, there also are millions of internally displaced people (e.g., in Colombia) and those who migrate to other countries in Latin America or elsewhere around the globe.

5. For fuller treatments, see M. Daniel Carroll R., *The Bible and Borders: Hearing God's Word on Immigration* (Grand Rapids: Brazos, 2020), 9–50; cf. Mark W. Hamilton, *Jesus, King of Strangers: What the Bible Really Says about Immigration* (Grand Rapids: Eerdmans, 2019).

Lines in the Sand: Struggling for Our *Latinidad*

The history of God's people begins with *Abram*. This patriarch was from Ur in the region of southern Babylonia, today southeastern Iraq, an important city and center of worship of the moon god. The book of Genesis does not tell us why Abram migrates. It simply recounts that he traveled northwest hundreds of miles with his father Terah, wife Sarai, and nephew Lot to Haran, close to what is now the Turkey-Syria border. After Terah's death, Abram and his family continued their migration to Canaan (Gen. 11:31–32), another journey of hundreds of miles. Both stages of their migration would have been arduous and largely on foot, replete with the dangers that characterized travel in the ancient world (such as robbery, the challenge of finding food and drink on the way for them and their animals, and illness). Abram left behind his country, kin, and father's house (12:1)—that is, everything that was familiar (society, culture, friends) and his extended family. By leaving his father's house, Abram also forfeited any claims to inheritance and social status. The decision to migrate would have been incredibly difficult and costly in many ways. Complicating matters was that he did not know his final destination, except that it would be in a distant land, unlike what he and those who went with him knew.

Not long after they arrived in Canaan, there was a severe famine (Gen. 12:10). Hunger made that migration to Canaan more unsettling, because Abram and his wife, Sarai, had to move again, this time to Egypt to look for food. They had to continue to migrate or perish. As they approached what may have been one of several Egyptian fortresses that guarded Egypt's eastern boundaries, they devised a disturbing scheme to survive: fearing violence, they lied to cross that borderland, and Sarai put her body at risk so that they could eat and potentially save her husband from being killed (12:11–15; cf. 20:11–13). Fear and desperation called for extreme measures. They had become strangers three times over, first in Haran, then in Canaan, and now in Egypt. Unprotected and vulnerable, yet resilient, they were willing to take risks for each other. In each step of their journeys, their stay depended on the benevolence of the host peoples.

Abram and Sarai eventually migrate back to Canaan (a fourth move!) and continue their seminomadic existence (Gen. 13:1–4). Only many years later does the old patriarch buy property, a field with a cave to bury his wife (23:3–20). After all this time, Abraham[6] confesses that he still feels like an outsider. In his negotiations for this plot of ground, Abraham clearly respects local customs and appreciates the people among whom he and his family dwell (and they admire him), but his heart tells him that his roots lie elsewhere. "I am a foreigner and stranger," he says to the Hittites (23:4 NIV).

The chapters in Genesis that chronicle Abraham's life recount that his experiences as a migrant were a training ground in faith. The patriarch is not an example of unwavering belief in God's promise to bless him with descendants and land (Gen. 12:1–3). Over the decades Abraham learns to trust in divine protection and provision. Sometimes he questions why things do not go like he hopes. There are episodes where he is willing to compromise Sarah's safety to protect himself (12:13–20; 20:2–13), and he allows for the tragic mistreatment of Hagar and their son, Ishmael (16:5–6; 20:8–14). Ironically, for cultural reasons, Sarah the migrant lashes out at the foreigner in their household. Yet there also

6. In Gen. 17:5, Abram (probably meaning "exalted father," perhaps in reference to God) is renamed Abraham (possibly "father of many"). I follow the biblical narrative in using "Abraham" in passages after 17:5. Sarai is renamed Sarah in 17:15. Both names apparently mean "princess."

are moments of stellar conviction and witness. Abram graciously cedes the choice of land to his nephew Lot (13:1–13) and then rescues him (14:13–16), blesses Melchizedek (14:17–24), and intercedes for God to have mercy on Sodom and Gomorrah (18:16–33). God twice commends him for his faith and confirms the original promise of 12:1–3 by word (15:6, 17–21; 22:15–18) and covenant (15:18; 17:4–14). This faith is noticed by Abimelech, who confesses that he sees the hand of God in Abraham's life (21:22–24)!

Several parts of the story are relevant for us, but here I highlight just a few. We will return to other dimensions in the next section. To begin with, like with the patriarch, there is much that Latinas and Latinos give up to migrate to this country. Leaving means disrupting family life, abandoning familiar cultural roots and language (both verbal and nonverbal), and forsaking who knows what possessions or property. For some, violence or extreme poverty trigger the move, and migrating is the only way to escape unlivable situations. Whatever the reason, the decision to leave everything behind is heart-wrenching. And then comes the trek north to the US. It can occur in several stages, with stops along the way, some fraught with danger of all kinds. Other uncertainties await at the border. Like Abram and Sarai, immigrants sometimes feel forced to make what seem like morally compromising choices to cross a border to realize their different future. Again, desperation can lead to desperate measures for those who have risked it all to make the journey.

If and when Latinas and Latinos are able to enter the US, there lies ahead yet another journey (or journeys) to a destination even farther from home and the life our families knew. Once there, wherever "there" may be, the bewildering process of engaging a broad range of cultural and legal challenges for family life, schooling, and work begins. These carry their own pressures and can raise doubts about the move itself. Was it a mistake? Even after years in the US, now enmeshed in this very different context and respecting its way of life and people, like the patriarch we may say, "I am a foreigner and stranger." Even after all the adjustments and redefining of who we are and what we do, we might wonder, "Do we belong?" What do these changes mean for us, our children, and our grandchildren? How do they impact our *latinidad*?[7]

In the midst of these disconcerting experiences, one thing that characterizes many Latinas and Latinos and their communities is their Christian faith.[8] There are all kinds of Latino/a churches, and the millions of attendees bolster the numbers of many denominations and the Catholic Church, even as the US as a whole becomes increasingly secularized. We will return to our faith and its impact on this country in the next chapter. At this point, the key is to recognize the importance of Christian faith to our culture. We need to highlight, too, that Abraham, the father of the faith, was an immigrant! His life was characterized by difficult physical journeys of migration, but these also functioned as a spiritual pilgrimage molded by those experiences and decisions, both good and bad. As Latinos and Latinas, we need to embrace the spiritual dimension and lessons of our journey and in our new situation and trust that God's hand is on us as we try to remain faithful to ourselves and our faith.

7. In "Aculteración e iglesia latina en los Estados Unidos," Juan Francisco Martínez Guerra offers five categories of Latinos/as in the US: the monocultural (insulated in immigrant communities), the bicultural (most are born or raised here), the marginal (occasional identification with their *latinidad*), the fleeing (don't negate their Latino/a identity but actively seek to assimilate), and the assimilated. Juan F. Martínez Guerra and Luis Scott, eds., *Iglesias peregrinas en busca de identidad: Cuadros del protestantismo en los Estados Unidos* (Buenos Aires: Kairós, 2004), 154–57.

8. See, e.g., "Religious Landscape Study: Latinos," Pew Research Center, 2014, https://www.pewresearch.org/religion/religious-landscape-study/racial-and-ethnic-composition/latino/.

Joseph was Jacob's favorite son, and Jacob was not subtle about his preference of Joseph over his brothers. Joseph's dreams of their bowing down to him sounded like arrogant gloating and made this obvious bias worse. His brothers hated him for it (Gen. 37:1–11). One day when Joseph checked on his brothers as they tended the family's flocks, they plotted to murder him. Instead of killing him, they sold Joseph to a passing caravan of traders headed to Egypt, who then sold him to Potiphar, one of Pharaoh's high-ranking officers (37:12–36). Joseph was what we call today a "forced migrant," a victim of vengeance and potential violence.

The first thing to notice in this story is Joseph's integrity and hard work. This quality earned him the privilege of being promoted to overseer of Potiphar's household (Gen. 39:1–6). Later, Joseph impresses everyone in prison, both the person in charge and his fellow prisoners (39:21–40:4). With God's help, Joseph interprets the dreams of other prisoners and, most famously, one of Pharaoh's. Not only does he reveal to Pharaoh the meaning of that dream; Joseph also gives him advice as to how to proceed. His character and wisdom so impress Pharaoh that he is released from prison and named governor over Egypt (41:37–41, 44)! He would navigate Egypt's economic challenges with great skill.

Joseph had integrated himself into Egyptian life in multiple ways. He learned the Egyptian language. He adapted to Egyptian customs (Gen. 41:14; 43:32) and protocols (41:42–43) and had an Egyptian wife (41:45). In fact, Joseph had so acclimated to his new context and its ways of dressing and grooming that his brothers did not recognize him until he revealed his identity to them (42:8; 45:1–15).

Through all of this, Joseph never abandoned his roots. To begin with, he gave his two sons Israelite names, not Egyptian ones (Gen. 41:50–52). Joseph also never forgot his mother tongue; he was bilingual (42:23–24). Joseph was concerned, too, about the welfare of his extended family back home. He secured their safe passage into Egypt, where he provided for them (45:9–11; 47:11–12, 27). He dearly loved his father Jacob and wanted to take care of him in his old age (46:28–30; 50:1). Once reunited with his extended family, Joseph unashamedly presented this old shepherd and some of his brothers to Pharaoh, even though Egyptians despised shepherds (47:7; cf. 43:32; 46:31–34). Family meant more than Egyptian social taboos. But Joseph had won the gratitude and admiration of Pharaoh, so his family was graciously received at the royal court (47:5–11; cf. 45:16–20). At the end of his own life, Joseph asked that his bones be taken back to his ancestral land (50:24–25)—*that* place was Joseph's true home.

Again, much in this story echoes our Latino/a experience. First, Joseph's character and hard work made an impression on the majority culture and its leadership, even though that culture loathed his people and family background. How true for our communities! We are known for being hard workers in everything we do and for contributing to society, even as some might discriminate against us and marginalize us in obvious or subtle ways.

Joseph has deep connections to his family and commits to look after them from his position of privilege in his new land. Family is central to our Latino/a culture, too, so this heartfelt obligation makes perfect sense to us. Like Joseph, we try to support family in our countries of origin and send remittances, and if family members are with us in this country, we try to help in any ways that we can. In Joseph's case, he is able to coordinate what legal jargon labels "family reunification" and bring his extended family to Egypt, something many Latinas and Latinos long to have the legal power to do for their families as well. Joseph also is fluent in the language of his parents and of the host country, so he is able to move between both cultures. Being bilingual and bicultural at some level is a gift that many of us also have; we have the skill to move back and forth across boundaries that those around us often cannot fathom or do not value.

As with Abraham, we also must not lose sight of the centrality of Joseph's faith. Even though he went through terrible experiences that were not his fault, God was with him (Gen. 39:2–5, 21). Joseph knows this and declares his trust in the Lord (40:8; 41:16, 25–32, 37–39, 51–52). Famously, Joseph forgives his brothers' betrayal because he had seen God's hand in his life (45:4–9; 50:20). Latinos and Latinas, too, are a spiritual people. We trusted God in the journey to this country (or came to know God through the journey), and we trust him now, at home and in our churches! *Dios está con nosotros* (God is with us). This does not mean that life here is easy or fair, but we believe in the God of Joseph.

Daniel and his three friends were taken away to Babylon before that empire invaded Judah, besieged the city of Jerusalem, and destroyed it (Dan. 1:1, 3–4). Babylonian foreign policy involved removing the best and brightest from conquered lands and training them for service to the empire, and this was the fate of Daniel and his friends. They were educated and from well-to-do families, and so they fit the ideal imperial profile.[9]

We need to appreciate what these young people endured. First, their names were changed. Their names, which reflected faith in the God of Israel (Daniel, Hananiah, Mishael, Azariah), were replaced with names related to Babylonian gods (Belteshazzar, Shadrach, Meshach, Abednego). These imposed labels would have been blas-

9. John J. Ahn, "Forced Migrations Guiding the Exile: Demarcating 597, 587, and 582 B.C.E.," in *By the Irrigation Canals of Babylon: Approaches to the Study of the Exile*, ed. John J. Ahn and Jill Middlemas, Library of Hebrew Bible/Old Testament Studies 526 (New York: Bloomsbury, 2012), 173–89.

phemous to them! Then, they were taught Babylonian literature, which would have been based largely on religious texts. This blasphemous material challenged their faith, too, with its different view of the world and of the divine. What made this situation even more difficult was the belief in the ancient world that military triumph was proof of the superiority of the gods of the victorious armies. In other words, the defeat of their home country, Judah, meant that the Babylonian gods were more powerful than the Lord; the God of their small nation had lost the war to the gods of the greatest empire in the world. And now, so far from home, could they continue believing in God? The vessels from the temple in Jerusalem also had been taken to the temple of the gods of Babylon as trophies of the empire's victory, a powerful statement of that "undeniable fact" of the supremacy of their gods. The entire vision of life of these young men was negated by what they heard, saw, and lived through.

Daniel and his friends had been robbed of everything. They had been forcefully taken to Babylon, probably making that journey of hundreds of miles on foot; they had lost loved ones in the war; their homes and social status had been destroyed; and now even their very identity had been taken away from them. All they held dear was gone. What would they have felt? Anger? Shame? Hopelessness? Confusion? Doubts? What kinds of trauma were they dealing with?[10]

The only space left to negotiate was their diet (Dan. 1:8–16). They could not negotiate their location, the curriculum, or their name change. They turned to their food, which was a strong

10. Trauma studies are a significant component of migration research today and in biblical studies. Note, e.g., the raw emotions in Ps. 137 of those recently deported to Babylon; the book of Lamentations depicts the distress of those who survived the horrific sacking of Jerusalem.

cultural marker for Jews. At the end of the allotted time for this food experiment, it was clear that it had worked; they were healthier than the others in training. What this brave stance meant was that, even though Babylon had taken away everything they held dear and even changed their names, they were still Jews![11] They had their food, and thus their identity. And, to everyone's surprise, they were better than any of the native born (1:20)! Daniel would go on to have a high position in government and serve under three kings (chaps. 3–6).

In Latino and Latina immigrant communities, we witness the constant negotiation with this country's larger culture. Often this is a negotiation of loss: loss of parts of our culture (such as our mother tongue and the nonverbal language of *el calor humano* [warm human interaction] that characterizes our greetings and goodbyes), of many ties back to our countries of origin, and of how we do family. In this negotiation of loss we feel overwhelmed as we try to find our own place in a world that pressures us in all kinds of ways to assimilate, to conform to *its* view of life. These tensions can play out in our homes and in our churches, as our young people sometimes wrestle with feeling ashamed of their past, the language of home, and even of parents who may not speak English well and who may seem out of touch, even while the parents themselves are trying to adjust to this environment without losing their identities and self-worth. In other words, each generation is grappling with how to live in this context as a minority. Trying to hold on to some of our roots is a lot of work. What do we have to give up to survive and succeed? How do we organize

11. This kind of strategy by powerless, subordinate groups is called a "hidden transcript," one that is full of significance that those in control miss. See James C. Scott, *Domination and the Arts of Resistance: The Hidden Transcript* (New Haven: Yale University Press, 1990).

our homes and parent our children in this context? Do we always have to lose in these unavoidable negotiations? What does it mean to be Latinos and Latinas in an Anglo world?

Food is a key cultural marker. It was for Daniel and his friends, and it is for us. Just look at all the restaurants and grocery stores in our communities and the potluck dinners or coffee times in our churches. This food lingers over the generations—*tamales, taquitos, empanadas, pupusas, frijol con arroz, horchata, posole,* sweet breads; I could go on. Each country will have brought its own favorites to the US. We share these delights across our national lines as an expression of *familia* and our *latinidad*. There is solidarity in our food. It is our stake in the ground.

Tragically, our young people sometimes deal with stereotypical caricatures about their abilities and potential, that they are somehow inferior to others. Daniel teaches us something fundamentally different and absolutely crucial. In this book we learn that we, like him, can be just as good as or better than majority culture kids! Even though we *are* different, we are just as smart and we will shine! To think that we are "less than" or limited is a destructive lie we need to confront and deny. Minority young people actually are the future of this country! This is an undeniable sociological and demographic fact.

Finally, Daniel and his friends, like Abraham and Joseph, were people of faith. Not only do they testify to their God in Daniel 1 in that food experiment, but later they are willing to die instead of bowing the knee to the golden image of Nebuchadnezzar (Dan. 3). Daniel puts up with religious mockery (Dan. 5) and a plot against him by jealous, prejudiced political rivals (Dan. 6). He and his friends live out their marginal status with confidence in God in spite of all they have lost and in spite of everything thrown at them. Their steadfast confidence in God was a powerful witness to the Babylonian kings (2:17–23, 46–47; 3:28–29; 4:34–37; 5:29; 6:25–27). We, too, must continue to grow in faith in that same God and be a strong testimony to the majority culture in which we live.

Probably the most well-known immigrant story in the Old Testament is found in the story of *Ruth*. From the opening verse of Ruth, this is an account about migration. Naomi, her husband, and their two sons migrate from Bethlehem in Judah across the Dead Sea to Moab. There was hunger in the land, and they move to survive (Ruth 1:1–2). There, the sons marry Moabite women, Ruth and Orpah (1:4). That is, these two Moabite women marry immigrants.

In time, Naomi's husband and sons die. In a very natural human response, Naomi wants to return to her home village. Apparently, things had gotten better there (Ruth 1:6). Orpah ends up staying in Moab, but Ruth accompanies her mother-in-law to Judah. Now Ruth is the immigrant.

Ruth's declaration to Naomi is famous, but what most miss is that Naomi says nothing in reply (Ruth 1:16–18). There is no "Thank you" or "Yes, we can do this together!" When they arrive in Bethlehem, the women come out to greet Naomi, only to hear her express bitterness over the loss of her husband and sons (1:19–21). She does not introduce the women to Ruth or even mention her. How awkward was that moment for Ruth? Naomi complained that she had returned empty from Moab . . . and there was Ruth, standing alone, perhaps silent off to the side, a Moabite.

Throughout the book, Ruth carries her ethnic label. To the reapers she is "the Moabite" (Ruth 2:6); to the people at the village gate, "the woman" (4:11) and "this young woman" (4:12); and to the other women, "your daughter-in-law" (4:15). The only one who says her name besides the narrator of the story is Boaz, but he always adds "the Moabite" (4:5, 10 NIV). She is a perpetual foreigner. The workers in the field do not know her name; they know her only by her hard work (2:5–7). Once again, the immigrant impresses everyone with an incredible work ethic; her loyalty to her Judean mother-in-law also is striking (2:11–12; 4:15).

Some of Ruth's struggles are unique to being a woman. Boaz warns her to be careful with the men in the field and stay close to the women reapers for her protection, advice repeated by Naomi (Ruth 2:8–9, 21–23). On her mother-in-law's direction she meets Boaz secretly at night on the threshing floor, something that could have permanently ruined her reputation in her new setting if things had turned out differently (3:14).

Boaz marries Ruth and they have a son, Obed (Ruth 4:13). When the baby is presented to Naomi and the women say to Naomi that this boy will take care of her in her old age, she still says nothing (4:14–15). But Naomi does take this little one in her arms; maybe now the Moabite Ruth will be totally embraced by her mother-in-law from Judah. Ruth constantly proves that she is brave, untiring, and resourceful. By the end of the story, she is praised by the elders of Bethlehem and the women who ignored her in the beginning as being like Israel's foremothers (4:11). Ruth had won over the entire town. Her son was of mixed heritage, with a Moabite mother and a father from Judah. The verses that close the book let readers know that from this bicultural son of a poor immigrant woman would come David, Israel's greatest king (4:18–22). We can assume that growing up in Bethlehem would be different for him than what his mother had experienced as a recently arrived immigrant woman.

There are innumerable stories of hardworking, self-sacrificing Latina immigrants, who face prejudice and exclusion as they do all they can to survive in their new setting. Perhaps like Ruth, their efforts to support their families may finally pay off. Like her, many Latinas marry men from the host culture and have bicultural children. That is my (Danny's) story: I am Obed, the son of a Guatemalan mother and a father from Boston (who was the son of Irish immigrants). There are a lot of Obeds now, and the number is growing! We have not had to go through what our mothers or our *abuelas* went through.

Mi mamá would tell me stories; they are not mine, but as I look back, I am so appreciative of all the things she did to instill in my brother and me an appreciation of our *latinidad*, more particularly of our *guatemalidad*. What Ruth also teaches us is that there is no *one* immigrant experience, no one-size-fits-all. There are those in more monocultural Latino/a families and many others of mixed marriages and upbringings. And yet we still share the immigrant story.

Notice that a child is the one who helped bridge the differences in that village of Bethlehem long ago. That often is the case today as well. It is through our children at school and on the soccer field that our families find points of contact and enter conversation with others. What is truly amazing is that from this immigrant woman came such a significant person in the history of Israel. One wonders how many momentous daughters and sons will be born to Latinas. We have no idea what their impact, our impact, will be on the history of this country! Through all the trials and tribulations, we can see the sovereign care of God taking us into a future we cannot imagine (Ruth 2:20; 3:10).

It Is All So Unfair: Exclusion and Exploitation

There can be all kinds of unfortunate realities to contend with in this new land, discrimination that outsiders inevitably face. Three Old Testament stories reflect some of the kinds of adversity that our people experience as immigrants and descendants of immigrants.

To start with, when Joseph was accused by Potiphar's wife of trying to rape her, whom did her husband and the authorities believe (Gen. 39:11–20)? The Egyptian woman or the foreigner? Joseph was the one who was sent to languish in prison. Years later under the new Pharaoh, when there was no living memory of Joseph, the text tells us that the Egyptians were frightened by the large and growing number of Israelites. The presence of so many of foreign descent made the Egyptians worry about their national security (Exod. 1:8–12). Their response was to exploit the Israelites as cheap labor (1:13–14). The barbaric next step to control this foreign population was Pharaoh's decree that newborn Israelite boys be killed. Only the courage and cunning of Israelite midwives saved these children (1:15–22).

Later, the Egyptians refused to provide the Israelites with straw for making bricks while keeping the quotas the same (Exod. 5:6–19). Straw was crucial for solidifying and stabilizing the mud bricks, so this new law made no economic sense. The Israelites were building Egyptian buildings, not anything for themselves. One would think that the Egyptians would want the best bricks possible in the most efficient way in the fastest time! Prejudice and fear had clouded their judgment and led to cruel and counterproductive policies. A harmful by-product of this oppression was that the Israelites had absorbed this view of themselves as dependent on the Egyptians. They were fearful and angry because the process to leave Egypt was triggering pushback and hardship in the short term (5:20; 6:9; 14:10–12); even after the exodus, they romanticized what life was like under the Egyptian yoke (16:2–3; 17:1–3). Said another way, the Israelites had absorbed that culture's untruths about who they were and what they were capable of being and doing.

I have already mentioned the hardships in Daniel 1. Daniel and his friends have to confront several kinds of disorientation, as well as the disadvantage of learning how to perform in another culture against others vying for position and prestige. The proposal concerning food, as well as the refusal of Daniel's friends to bow before the golden statue of Nebuchadnezzar (Dan. 3:8–24) and Daniel's demeanor before an arrogant Belshazzar (5:13–29), required deep inner fortitude. In addition, Daniel had to deal with the envy of political leaders. They could not find grounds for attacking his integrity (6:1–5), so they conspired for the king to pass a law that they knew would compromise the practice of Daniel's faith and condemn him to an awful death (6:6–18). That plan was divinely thwarted, and Daniel was not devoured by lions (6:19–23).

We do not see overt prejudice in the story of Ruth. Things are more subtle. She is almost invisible to the men in the fields (Ruth 2), and the danger to her reputation at the threshing floor would have been more serious because she was a foreigner (Ruth 3). When she first interacts with Boaz, she calls herself a *nokriyyah* (2:10), the pejorative term for a foreigner, although she qualified as a *ger*, the label for a more welcomed outsider who has come to live in Israel. Is this a reflection of how she felt in her new surroundings? Had she picked up covert signals indicating that she was an undesired outsider? After all, she was a Moabite, a people despised by Israel (e.g., Deut. 23:3–4). She benefited from Israelite laws, like being able to gather in the fields as the widow of an Israelite and as a foreigner (24:19–22), and the marriage to Boaz was connected to the custom of Levirate marriage (25:5–10). This welcomed legal support, however, may not have lessened how people may have perceived her or how she felt.[12]

12. For the various terms used for foreigners in the Old Testament and the laws designed to respond to their needs, see Carroll R., *Bible and Borders*, 56–83.

So much in this story sounds familiar. Many Latinos and Latinas can relate to being on the receiving end of prejudice—both veiled and blatant, some of which can have legal ramifications— and to feeling out of place, under suspicion because we have different roots, have our own customs, and may speak another language. Many of our people also experience exploitation in the workplace, where they are underpaid, not offered benefits, and do not have job protection (it is not difficult to point to examples in landscaping, construction, and many service industries). There is also the danger of Latinos and Latinas, especially our young people, absorbing the stereotypes that the larger culture imposes on us. Yet, in spite of inequity and intolerance, Latinas and Latinos are demonstrating amazing strength, resilience, and resourcefulness.

What can drive this unfair treatment of Latinos and Latinas is fear: fear of change, fear of shifting cultural dynamics, and fear of an unfamiliar foreign presence that is perceived to be a threat to local safety and national security. Of course, this country does not have a monolithic culture. Black Harlem, the deep Anglo South, Polish neighborhoods in Chicago, Iowa farmers of Dutch descent, New Orleans Cajuns, SoCal surfers, and on and on . . . there is no *one* American culture. The US is a collection of many cultures, many with their own immigrant histories, customs, and foods. Sadly, those histories reveal the same fears and biases in the past that Latinos and Latinas endure today. But we are adding new and wonderful things to this grand cultural mix.

We Are Here!

The Old Testament offers a rich resource for Latinas and Latinos as individuals and for our communities. There we find stories of God's people millennia ago who migrated to new lands, willingly or because they were forced to, and experienced things similar to what Latinos and Latinas go through as immigrants or as descendants of immigrants. There we read of tribulations in Canaan, Egypt, and Babylon. But these immigrants persevered in spite of those hardships and were able to maintain their identity at some level and witness to faith in God.

These biblical stories can—they must!—serve us as *counter-narratives* to the stories that many want to tell of us. Those ancient immigrants lived in ways that contradicted what those around them believed about them and tried to do to them. As these stories become *our* counter-narratives, they can inspire us to endure, survive, and succeed *as Latinos and Latinas* in *our* time and place. They offer models of struggling for life with hard work, integrity of character, and deep faith. How this might play itself out within our own families and specific contexts will differ, but through these stories we take heart in our rich *latinidad* and spiritual commitments.

There is a growing body of literature of Latino and Latina immigrant experiences in the US as our people remember family stories and speak of the frustrations, fears, and achievements. People from Mexican, Puerto Rican, Cuban, Guatemalan, Salvadoran, and other backgrounds are opening their hearts to tell tales of leaving, arriving, and integrating into neighborhoods, schools, and jobs.[13] There are volumes relating the hardships of the trek to *el Norte*.[14] Of course, sociological, political, and cultural studies

13. The list of authors of first- and second-generation Latin American roots is long and growing. A sampling could include Julia Álvarez, Sandra Cisneros, Sonia Nazarío, Francisco Goldman, Cristina Henríquez, and Marcelo Hernández Castillo, among many others. Christian authors, like Sarah Quezada and Karen González, are weaving their faith into their personal stories. These are authors who write in English, but there also is literature in Spanish being published in the various countries of origin.

14. A key name, again among many others, is Luis Alberto Urrea (*The Devil's Highway, Into the Beautiful North, The House of Broken Angels*). A powerful

abound, and university departments are being founded to help grapple with these realities. And then there is our music that sings about the trip north (such as the Mexican *corridos*) and our blues, and the movies that portray our souls.

All of this is necessary and good—and often uncomfortable—as we work to define our place, highlight our contributions . . . and sort out our *latinidad* in this country. In this process, let us remember the voice of the Word of God, its stories that accompany us on this journey. *La Palabra de Dios nos acompaña en este peregrinaje* (the Word of God accompanies us in this pilgrimage).

---

book is Óscar Martínez's *The Beast: Riding the Rails and Dodging Narcos on the Migrant Trail*, trans. Daniela María Ugaz and John Washington (New York: Verso, 2013). This title does not do justice to the original title in Spanish (2010): *Los migrantes que no importan* (*The Migrants Who Don't Matter*).

4

A Latino/a Blessing

Old Testament II

The preceding chapter looked at immigrant stories in the Old Testament. They were just a sampling; more could have been included, such as those of Isaac and Jacob, Moses, Jeremiah, Ezekiel, Esther, and others. I shared those stories for two reasons. On the one hand, they reveal how central migration is to the history of the people of God. Even though some in the US view immigrants from Latin America negatively, it is possible to see their presence in this country as a blessing and a gift from God. Millions of believers have come north, and many others have come to faith after their arrival. In other words, this movement can be appreciated as another chapter in the history of the migration of God's people, one that stretches back to biblical times. Migration has been central to the spread of the good news and to the growth of the Christian church for millennia, and we are witnessing this here in real time.[1]

In addition, these individuals in the Old Testament experienced challenges of surviving and flourishing in strange lands that are analogous to what Latino/a immigrants and their families face. Those stories become ours. The people in those stories are *compañeros* and *compañeras* (companions) in our Latino/a journeys to and within the US.

This chapter turns to how the Old Testament can provide a sense of purpose to Latino and Latina believers, revealing that we are *participants* and *protagonists* in God's mission within the US and beyond. Even as Latinos/as sort out discrimination and obstacles in our lives, we need to appreciate a biblical framework that can help us visualize life here self-consciously as Christians. Two passages will serve as a lens to process life as a minority, a minority within this society as a whole and within the broader Christian church here. I then return to the stories from the prior chapter to see how those migrant followers of God lived out their faith for others and how their example can encourage Latinos and Latinas today.

Back to the Beginning

The first passage for grounding our self-perception is Genesis 12. It comes at an important point in the biblical narrative. Humanity seems without hope. The entire world is violent and in rebellion against God (Gen. 6:5–6, 11–12). There are glimpses of a few

1. Jehu J. Hanciles, *Migration and the Making of Global Christianity* (Grand Rapids: Eerdmans, 2021); Sadiri Joy Tira and Tetsunao Yamamori, eds., *Scattered and Gathered: A Global Compendium of Diaspora Missiology*, rev. ed. (Carlisle: Langham Global Library, 2020).

individuals who do seek God (4:26; 5:22), but ultimately all of humanity is judged (chaps. 6–8). Even Noah, the one who looked like he would be the one to reverse the curse of Genesis 3 ("He will comfort us in the labor and painful toil of our hands caused by the ground the LORD has cursed," 5:29 NIV) and whose very name underscores that point,[2] fails dramatically. The last we see of Noah, he is drunk, passed out in his tent (9:20–21). So much for the hope of the world!

Then comes the building of the Tower of Babel (Gen. 11). Once again, the whole earth has turned its back on God, refusing now to fulfill the mandate to fill the earth (11:4; cf. 1:28). Instead, they build a tower to try to connect with the heavens to make a name for themselves.[3] The potential for evil of a united and defiant humanity, however, knows no bounds, so the Lord disperses them (11:6–9). This divine action explains how the descendants of the three sons of Noah, the peoples listed in chapter 10, were scattered across the known world of that time according to their clans, languages, and territories (10:5, 20, 31–32). In the biblical narrative, all nations are born at Babel, with that seed of arrogance in their hearts.

The call of Abram (Gen. 12:1–3), which is our focus, comes right after the account of the Tower of Babel.[4] These verses are significant for several reasons. The first thing to notice is the centrality

---

2. Noah in Hebrew is *Noah*, a wordplay on the verb *naham* ("bring relief" or "comfort") in this verse and the verb *nuah*, "to rest."

3. Most likely the tower would have been a ziggurat, a stair-shaped structure. Scholars debate whether it was designed so that humans could access the heavens or whether it was to serve as a way for the deity to descend to the earth. See John H. Walton, "Genesis," in *Zondervan Illustrated Bible Backgrounds Commentary* 1 (Grand Rapids: Zondervan, 2009), 60–65.

4. For a helpful exposition, see Christopher J. H. Wright, *The Mission of God: Unlocking the Bible's Grand Narrative* (Downers Grove, IL: IVP Academic, 2006), 194–220. See there, too, discussion of "will be blessed" in 12:3 (cf. 18:18; 22:18; 26:4–5; 28:14). Some translate this verb as "will bless themselves."

of the concept of *bless/blessing*. The noun or verb appears five times:[5]

> [2]I will make you into a great nation,
>   and I will *bless* you;
> I will make your name great,
>   and you will be a *blessing*.[6]
> [3]I will *bless* those who *bless* you,
>   and whoever curses you I will curse;
> and all peoples on earth
>   *will be blessed* through you. (12:2–3 NIV)

What does "to bless" mean? "Bless" and "blessing" are common spiritual or church words that we use but rarely define. We say, "God bless you" (*qué el Señor te bendiga*) or "we are blessed" (*somos bendecidos*) and smile and nod in agreement without asking what this actually means! Genesis clarifies its significance for us. The verb occurs in the creation account in 1:22, 1:28, and 2:3 (cf. 5:2; 9:1). There, it is linked to productive life for all creatures, nonhuman and human alike. In 2:3, the seventh day, or Sabbath, is blessed and set aside for God. That is—and this is important—divine blessing is both physical and spiritual: it refers to creaturely things we can enjoy, as well as a space for a relationship with the God of creation. An incredible blessing, indeed!

In the book of Genesis, we see the blessing theme unfold as the patriarchs have children, see their flocks multiply, find water for themselves and their animals, and live in peace with others. These are all material blessings of family and livelihood. But we

5. The verb and noun clearly are important for Genesis. They appear over eighty times!

6. This line can also be read with an imperative force: "and be a blessing."

also read that they build altars, call out to God, and testify of the Lord before the people among whom they live. In other words, they experience the full blessing of God and share it with their neighbors. Their presence brings prosperity to others (e.g., 30:29–30; 39:3–6), some of whom come to recognize the hand of God in their lives (e.g., 26:28–29).

Four other crucial things stand out in Genesis 12:1–3. To begin with, verse 2 tells us that the people of God are to be a blessing to others because God has blessed them. The word order in this line is fundamental: *because* we are blessed, we can (and are commanded to) be a blessing. Second, the name of the people of God will become great as we fulfill this mandate to bless others. That is, our greatness is based on faithfulness to God, not on self-promotion or vainglory based on some human achievement (like building an impressive tower!). This is a different way of understanding our worth; it is rooted in God's mission.

Third, verse 3 teaches us that the people of God are to be the instruments, or channel, of God's rich blessing to all peoples. This is the very reason for the creation of the people of God; we are here as God's hand and feet, as God's voice to call the nations to embrace the goodness of God. Fourth, verse 3 also reveals that the people of God should expect that others look down on us; some will discredit and despise us as we participate in God's work.

There is much here to unpack as Latino/a Christians, both individually and as churches. At the very least, we should learn to trust that God's desire is to bless us in all kinds of ways, materially and spiritually. This will happen, even as we encounter hardship in the course of everyday life (just look at how hard things were for the patriarchs and their families in the book of Genesis!). We can say "amen" to this! In our churches we constantly hear *testimonios*, the stories our brothers and sisters tell of the grace of God they experience as they try to navigate the challenges of life in this country. In other words, trusting in the blessing of God does not mean ignoring or minimizing the difficulties and unfairness of life as Latinos and Latinas; it does mean believing that God is with us in the midst of all of that.

Then comes the biblical text's instruction: because we have been blessed, we are to be a blessing to those around us. What might this mean? How is this to be done? We will return to this calling later in the chapter. As we will see, Latinas and Latinos are doing amazing things for the Lord. We are blessing others and are gaining a name for ourselves in our impact on Christian witness, church planting, outreach, theological reflection, and more. We are here for a purpose.

The last thing to take away from verse 3 is that Latinos and Latinas should expect that we will not always be well-received as we fulfill that call to be a blessing. As we try to live out our lives as Christians in this society, many face biases and misunderstandings because of our heritage, culture, and (perhaps) legal status. We may endure discrimination—being disparaged and dismissed, *menospreciados*, because of our *latinidad*—as we try to act on the divine mandate to be a blessing in this country. This is an additional layer of difficulty that we might bear that other Christians might not. Being a Latino/a Christian may not always be easy!

Life in a Strange Land

The second foundational passage is found in Jeremiah 29, in the letter that the prophet sent to the people from Judah who had been taken away to Babylon. The letter is addressed to the leaders of the exiled community and to the people in general (Jer. 29:1–3). The questions that the exiles naturally were asking themselves would have been, "What kind of life should we make for ourselves, so far away from home? How long will we be here? Will we eventually go back to Judah?" Jeremiah's advice begins at verse 4.

As we approach this passage, we need to recognize that the exiled community had no power. Judah already was under the Babylonian thumb, even as the devastating blow of the final invasion and Jerusalem's terrible devastation still lay a few years in the future.[7] They found themselves in a society that was quite strange in terms of its culture, laws, economic and political systems, and language. Theirs definitely was a minority presence within the most powerful empire on earth. More troubling, in the mindset of the ancient world (as we saw with Daniel in the previous chapter), Judah's defeat signaled their God's defeat. The gods of Babylon, not Yahweh, ruled the world. Did removal from their homeland also mean that Yahweh was no longer with them? Even if Yahweh were, what could he do after seemingly being unable to protect Judah from serious harm and its people from forced deportation?

The prophet gives the exiles constructive advice for surviving and thriving in that place. His words begin with "Thus says the LORD of hosts, the God of Israel" (Jer. 29:4 NRSV). Whatever they might think or whatever their circumstances would suggest, their God was there to guide and accompany them. Yahweh was not powerless or absent; they were still God's people. The exiles should not let their situation in that new context convince them of things that were not true about their God or about who they were.

The exiles are told to build homes, plant gardens, and eat their produce (Jer. 29:5). This is not a recommendation for the short

7. This letter would have been sent after 597 BCE, when Jerusalem was captured by Babylon, and many sent into exile (cf. 2 Kings 24:10–17). Jerusalem was destroyed in 587/586 BCE.

term. Building houses, sowing seed, and enjoying what their gardens would eventually yield would take years. To marry and establish families also speaks to living in that foreign land for generations (29:6). Jeremiah's words were pragmatic: the people were to secure places to live, ensure means of providing food for themselves, and safeguard the continuation of the community through family life and bearing children. These activities are the stuff of daily life, *lo cotidiano*. In other words, in investing in this new place, the exiles also were investing in their own well-being and prosperity and that of their children and their children's children.

At this juncture, the Genesis 12 pattern of being a blessing can come into play. Having benefited from the good hand of God, even though they had suffered the terrible trials of war and displacement, the exiles were to turn their attention to their new setting. Their God had not forgotten them. Yahweh's purpose was still to grant them *shalom*. They certainly needed to be assured of that after what they had been through. But God's *shalom* also was for others, even for the people of the empire that had defeated their country and deported them to Babylon! In fact, the exiled community was to actively *seek* that city's welfare, its *shalom* (Jer. 29:7).

Shalom is a Hebrew word that signifies a setting of peace. This absence of conflict is characterized by material prosperity, long life, and general communal well-being.[8] This exiled community of outsiders was to try to foster all these things in that strange land for themselves and others. They would benefit from contributing to that broader good: "In its *shalom* you will find your *shalom*" (Jer. 29:7). This participation in their new surroundings, the prophet says, was to include prayer on Babylon's behalf; in other words,

---

8. Philip J. Nel, "*šlm*," *New International Dictionary of Old Testament Theology and Exegesis*, ed. Willem A. VanGemeren (Grand Rapids: Zondervan, 1997), 4:130–35.

this mandate had a spiritual dimension. Their participation in their new context was to involve work, family life, and prayer.

This letter exhorts the exiles and their descendants to choose responsible and productive life as witnesses to their faith and to their culture. They were not to see themselves solely as victims of injustice (even though they surely were that) or allow themselves to be defined by how the empire might perceive of them as a defeated people. They also were not to buy into the worldview and values of the empire. In God's eyes, that would be a false and destructive take on life, even if legitimated by its government and false gods. They had to believe that Yahweh had plans of *shalom* for them, that a hopeful future lay ahead—in their case to return to their homeland (Jer. 29:11). As they experienced God's *shalom* in the present and sought the *shalom* of Babylon, they could rest assured that there was more *shalom* to come. This reworking of a mindset and priorities in a foreign land would not have been easy. There would be so much to learn and to overcome, especially at the beginning.

What might seeking the welfare of Babylon have looked like day to day, week after week, month after month? Jeremiah's letter does not say. It would need to be worked out continually by the exilic community. It would have required creativity, resourcefulness, discernment, and perseverance, depending on any host of factors in the various situations where the exiles found themselves. This would have been true for that first generation of exiles, and probably in different ways for their children and grandchildren. In spite of the challenges, in doing this they would fashion a positive future for themselves.

Being without power and status, then, did not mean having no say in what their lives might look like or having no impact on Babylon. The prophet assured them that there was hope at the margins, in a setting that at first may have seemed hopeless. In fact, we have archaeological data that reveal that some exiled families did well in Babylon. In addition, a Jewish community, descendants of those who had been forcibly removed to Babylon (today, modern Iraq), flourished there for centuries. That area would house a significant Jewish population until the regime of Saddam Hussein in the late twentieth century.

Something else that does not surface in this passage is that the exile was a place of fresh revelation from God. This community would be the source of a large portion of the Scripture. They produced several of our prophetic books, wrote psalms and some of the Old Testament historical books, and perhaps other parts of the Old Testament as well. In other words, their migrant realities were an incredibly fertile ground for theological reflection that, amazingly, continues to speak to believers around the globe today. In that strange land of Babylon, that immigrant community had to process what it meant to believe that Yahweh was active among them even though they were far from their homeland, that their God was indeed in control of what they had experienced and of where history was going, that they could worship in that context in new ways without a temple, and that they could trust that they could flourish as a vulnerable minority in spite of their losses. There, in Babylon, they received new revelation from God and fresh insights into the Lord's character and ways. Those different circumstances expanded their faith. This truly was *teología en el camino* and *en conjunto*! This appreciation of God and the life of faith only could have surfaced in *that* place and only *after* what they had been through.

Like with Genesis 12, there is much in this passage for Latinas and Latinos. Its potential was realized years ago by Latino pastor-theologian Eldin Villafañe. In his classic book *Seek the Peace of the*

City, a title that obviously echoes this passage, Villafañe speaks of a "Jeremiah Paradigm" for urban ministry.[9] Basing himself on the prophet's words, he encourages the Latino/a community in the US to critically engage the majority culture, to have a participatory presence that pursues the fullness of peace at both personal and social levels. The call to prayer in the prophet's letter is also important, Villafañe says. Prayer is needed to strengthen our community, to sustain it so as to be able to realize the impact God desires.

How this is to be navigated, of course, differs according to context and circumstances. There is no assurance that the complicated, ongoing processes of adjustments in families, schools, the workplace, and the broader social world of this country will not bring challenges. Like those ancient believers in Babylon, though, today Latinos and Latinas need to demonstrate creativity and diligent steadfastness, even as we are already doing! Often this can be hard, but through this prophetic word we learn that there is a *propósito* (a purpose) for our community in this country that goes beyond day-to-day survival strategies, as we strive in God's grace and sovereignty toward a new *mañana* (tomorrow). We, too, will learn to invest in our homes, family, and work here and seek the wider *shalom* of God in this society. As we are blessed, we can bless others.

Latino/a contributions to the US are evident everywhere—in all kinds of jobs and professions, higher education, government, every form of entertainment, multiple sports, literature, food, and much more. The Latino/a community is now the largest minority in the country with over sixty-two million in 2021, or almost 20 percent of the population. Latinos and Latinas make up about 20 percent of college students as well. And these percentages are

9. Eldin Villafañe, *Seek the Peace of the City: Reflections on Urban Ministry* (Grand Rapids: Eerdmans, 1995), 1–3.

growing. The future of this country inescapably will be shaped by our people.

The same holds true for the Christian church. We will close this chapter with a few examples of the Jeremiah Paradigm, but here I highlight that this *tierra ajena* (foreign land) is a fruitful setting for church, ministry, and witness in many ways. There are several large associations of Latino/a churches, such as NaLEC (National Latino Evangelical Coalition) and the NHCLC (National Hispanic Christian Leadership Conference). Every denomination, including the Roman Catholic Church, is benefiting from the influx of Latino/a Christians, and all are working to prepare leadership programs to meet this new reality.

Latinos and Latinas are producing a wide range of pastoral and theological work at many levels. This is part of our wider blessing. There are Latino/a Christian magazines, conferences of all kinds, and musicians. An array of English-language publishing houses is actively seeking Latino and Latina authors, even as several Spanish-language publishing houses and the Spanish-language divisions of English-language publishers thrive. As in Old Testament times, our migration experiences and the processes of adaptation to the majority sociocultural life as a minority are a rich seedbed for generating fresh thinking about God and ministry, Christian discipleship, and more. These reflections range from personal, lay-level accounts of our pilgrimages of faith as strangers in a strange land to pastoral helps on multiple topics to serious academic monographs. Our churches are largely Pentecostal or can have a Pentecostal flavor, so that tradition marks much of what is being done, but there also is a growing profile in some Latino/a circles of more Reformed theology. Churches and theology are budding within and beyond classic Christian traditions and expressions. Latinos and Latinas are bringing innovative wine in need of new wineskins to expand and enrich theology and practices within the American church and of the church in society.

A significant voice birthed in Latin American evangelical thinking called *la misión integral* (integral mission) is finding resonance among Latinos/as in this country.[10] This holistic/integral mission is defined by wedding the call to share the good news of forgiveness from personal sin with the obligation to oppose systemic injustice, and so more genuinely to incarnate gospel fidelity. Unlike some evangelical thinking of the majority culture, *la misión integral* does not bifurcate the spiritual from the compassionate. Important contributions are surfacing. They are not to be categorized simply as occupying "another place at the table" of pastoral and theological reflection within the expansive landscape of majority culture Christians, as just one of the many alternative ways of looking at God, the church, and the life of faith among the many that are on offer in our postmodern, postcolonial world. Or, even more frustratingly, these contributions should not be stereotyped pejoratively as co-opted evangelical standard bearers and then marginalized outside more prominent mainstream minority scholarship.[11]

No, these thinkers and practitioners represent the growing, diverse, grassroots Latino/a local churches that number in the tens of thousands across the denominational spectrum and beyond set

10. This theology was born within the Fraternidad Teológica Latinoamericana, begun in 1970. Founders included René Padilla (Ruth's father), Samuel Escobar, Pedro Arana, and my former colleague in Guatemala, Emilio Antonio Núñez. See Daniel Salinas, *Taking Up the Mantle: Latin American Evangelical Theology in the 20th Century* (Carlisle: Langham Global Library, 2017); cf. Robert Chao Romero, *Brown Church: Five Centuries of Latina/o Social Justice, Theology, and Identity* (Downers Grove, IL: IVP Academic, 2020), 154–62, 174–206.

11. This is not to diminish key contributions of mainline Latino/a scholars but instead to point out that they sometimes may not represent the commitments and convictions of evangelical and Pentecostal Latino/a believers.

ecclesial structures. Among these congregations, associations of churches, and institutions, the doing of theology is inseparable from the faith journeys of *la vida cotidiana* of millions of ordinary Latino/a believers and their families, at a remove from some of the concerns and jargon of the academy. A younger generation of Latinos and Latinas is coming on the scene that both is loyal to their local church and desires to pursue an authentic, contextualized, and relevant Latino/a theology that is rooted in strong convictions about the Scriptures and historic Christian faith. To identify and nurture these nascent expressions in today's complex and confusing Latino/a evangelical world will not be easy, but the future holds much promise. All of this, biblically, is connected to the charge of realizing our *shalom* and that of American society.

To sum up, two Old Testament passages, Genesis 12 and Jeremiah 29, provide a lens through which to understand the presence and role of Latino and Latina believers and our churches in the US. As God's people, we experience the good hand of God in the midst of trying circumstances. The divine call is to then bless those around us and to seek their *shalom*. This is not a pietistic escape or a passive acceptance of negative realities. Not at all. Rather, this framework contends that the various things we do, whether as individuals or as churches, as advocates for social transformation as natural extensions of *la misión integral*, or in whatever other capacity and activity, be understood as part of a divine mandate to contribute to the common good in God's name for the benefit of God's people and of the country as a whole.

Faithful Strangers and Theologians

Do the stories of the four individuals (Abram/Abraham, Joseph, Ruth, Daniel) whom we highlighted in the preceding chapter reflect the kind of perspective that this chapter proposes? Did those immigrants experience God's blessing and then extend it to those around them? I argue that they did, in their words and in their actions.

Our first biblical character was *Abram/Abraham*. He received that missional call of Genesis 12, and there began the accounts of how the patriarchs fulfilled that charge. Clearly, there are moments in Abraham's life when he does not live out what had been expected of him. His life of faith was complicated, with its ups and downs. Some less-than-stellar incidents were mentioned in the preceding chapter. But there are also moments when he was commended by God (however much his faith was always a work in progress!).

In Genesis 15 Abram wonders aloud to God how the promise of descendants could ever be fulfilled. The only apparent solution at hand is his servant Eliezer. Yahweh reassures him that the promise of a son holds, and Abram believes, and "he credited it to him as righteousness" (15:6 NIV). After instructing the patriarch to bring animals for a prescribed ritual, God brings on him a deep sleep and makes a covenant with Abram that reaffirms that promise (15:8–18). Years later, after the birth of Isaac, Abraham follows God's instructions to offer his only son as a sacrifice. His confidence that Yahweh would provide a sacrifice earns Abraham high praise that includes the words "I will surely bless you" (22:17 NIV). When Abraham's servant speaks to Laban about securing Rebekah as Isaac's wife, he declares how his master has been abundantly blessed of God (24:34–36).

The patriarch, forged through all kinds of testing and blessed in many ways, blesses others. For instance, Abram grants his nephew Lot first choice of land for pasture and then rescues him from being taken captive (Gen. 13–14), and he pleads for God's mercy upon Sodom and Gomorrah (18:22–33). In response to what he has seen, Abimelech declares, "God is with you [Abraham] in everything you do" (21:22 NIV), and the two make a covenant of peace (22:25–34). Later, we see the mutual respect and appreciation between Abraham the sojourner (23:4) and Ephron the Hittite, with whom the patriarch secures a place to bury his wife, Sarah (23:5–20).

Joseph extends blessings to others at familial and national levels. After enduring several misfortunes, he emerges as second in Egypt, well-placed in the royal court. The end result of the ensuing drama of the exchanges with Joseph's brothers who had come for food is the invitation to bring their families and their aged father Jacob to Egypt so that he could provide for them during the famine (45:9–11). The invitation is accompanied by concrete measures to facilitate that move from Canaan; he sends along wagons and provisions with his brothers for the journey back (45:16–25). Joseph's extended family settles in Goshen, a fertile area in the Nile delta, where they prosper (47:11–12; 48:27; 50:21).

Joseph's acts of blessing extend beyond his family. He organizes Egypt to withstand the seven-year famine, utilizing his administrative skills to benefit the nation.[12] The Egyptians clearly hold Joseph in high esteem, so his family receives a generous welcome from Pharaoh (45:16–21; 47:5–10). When Jacob dies, Joseph asks for and receives permission to bury his father back in Canaan; some Egyptians even accompany him on that trip (50:5–14). His wider blessings had generated a deep appreciation that benefited him and his family.

On several occasions *Daniel* gives words of insight to Babylonian and Persian kings, sometimes as rebuke. His wisdom and

12. Ironically and tragically, however, Joseph's policies facilitated the creation of Pharaoh's oppressive regime of the early chapters of the book of Exodus.

that of his three friends were unparalleled (Dan. 1:20). Daniel is revered as an interpreter of dreams of the true God (2:46–49); the courage of his friends is praised by Nebuchadnezzar, and their God is honored (3:28–30); this king acknowledges their God after his humiliation (4:34–37); Belshazzar applauds Daniel after he interprets the handwriting on the wall (5:29); and Darius commends Daniel and his God after he survives the lions' den (6:25–28). Throughout these chapters, extreme trials of faith redound to the glory of the Most High God in the mouths of the kings. Daniel and his friends are promoted for their perseverance and trust in God.

The lives of Abraham and Joseph are the vehicles of revelation and serve as exemplars of faith, but here there is more. The book of Daniel provides words pregnant with lasting truth in the proclamations and prayers of Daniel and his friends. They serve as a theological critique of empire. This is another example of theology arising out of exile, a theology in this case that exposes the limitations, the cruelty, and the just end of human arrogance. This is a migrant theology for the ages.

Our last case study is the book of *Ruth*, and only a few observations are in order. First, the underlying theme of the book about this immigrant Moabite is lovingkindness or loyal love (Hebrew: *ḥesed*). Naomi prays that God's loyal love be manifest in the life of her daughters-in-law, just as they had shown it to her and their dead husbands (Ruth 1:8); Naomi praises the Lord for not forgetting his loyal love by providing her and Ruth with a kinsman-redeemer in Boaz (2:20); and Boaz praises Ruth for her loyal love to Naomi and for her character (3:10). These are acts of blessings based on the mutual obligations of the women, Boaz, and God to assist others in need.

Second, this little book highlights the perseverance of a widowed peasant woman. She leaves behind her people and homeland to accompany her Israelite mother-in-law to Judah, where Moabites were not always welcome. She embraces Naomi's faith (1:16) and then works hard to secure their survival (2:6–7, 11–12, 17–18, 23). She risks a night meeting with Boaz (3:7–14), marries him, and is praised by everyone in the village. To the surprise of the reader, from that union will come Obed, ancestor of King David (4:18–20). Ruth is an amazing *mujer* (woman), whose strength of character is a blessing to her mother-in-law, her new family, and Bethlehem, and, in time, to the entire nation, forever.

The individuals in these four cases are blessed by God in particular ways as they experience the hardships of life, some that would have been inevitable for everyone in those settings but also some because they were outsiders. Their testimony of faith became strong, and they positively impacted those around them. We witness, in other words, these immigrants exemplifying the Genesis 12 / Jeremiah 29 pattern of receiving the goodness of God that then radiates outward in word and deed to their immediate context and now to us. They provide a precedent to encourage Latinos and Latinas in this country.

Blessing in Actual Time

The purpose of this chapter has been to reframe our strategies of survival and awareness of the challenges and injustices that Latinos and Latinas face within a constructive sense of why God has us here. However or whenever we or our families came to the US, however much we must deal with, there is a reason for our presence. *Nuestra presencia tiene propósito en los planes de Dios* (our presence has a purpose in the plans of God).

In this closing section I briefly profile three Latino/a churches in the greater Chicago area that are doing amazing things within their respective communities. These churches are different in size, setting, and focus. There is no one model of a Latino/a church; the diversity across the country is immense. This is to be expected given the multiple realities faced by first-, second-, and third-generation Latino/a congregations.[13] These three churches cannot represent that breadth. They do, however, provide examples of the Genesis 12 / Jeremiah 29 principle that couples being blessed with blessing others.

New Life Community Church is located in La Villita (Little Village), a historic Latino/a part of the city sometimes called the "Mexico of the Midwest." It is one of over twenty campuses of a multisite church, New Life Centers, in the city. The pastor, Paco (Luis) Amador, is originally from Mexico and has pastored this church for eighteen years. Every Sunday there are two services in Spanish and one in English, for which half of the attendees are Latinos and Latinas who prefer English. There also is an afternoon service in Q'eqchi', the language of an indigenous group from Guatemala of the same name. Hundreds have moved into the South Lawndale area and, because there is nothing in that language in Chicago, that church service has fostered relationships that are generating community in a foreign land.

In addition to offering traditional church activities, the church is closely connected to a nonprofit that runs a food depository across the street called Pan de Vida (Bread of Life). The Greater Chicago Food Depository selected the nonprofit and the church as community-based partners to coordinate the distribution of food to hundreds of needy families. New Vecinos (New Neighbors) is

13. See, e.g., Daniel A. Rodríguez, *A Future for the Latino Church: Models for Multilingual, Multigenerational Hispanic Congregations* (Downers Grove, IL: IVP Academic, 2011); Mark T. Mulder, Aída I. Ramos, and Gerardo Marti, *Latino Protestants in America: Growing and Diverse* (Lanham, MD: Rowman & Littlefield, 2017).

another outreach of this nonprofit. It addresses the housing challenges of recently arrived immigrants and delivers three hot meals
daily to police stations that are accommodating hundreds of new
arrivals who have been bused north from the US-Mexico border,
for whom no alternative venues are available.

The second church, Iglesia del Pueblo, is situated in West Chicago, which also is largely Latino/a. It is the Spanish congregation
of Wheaton Bible Church, a large suburban, predominantly Anglo
church. Around eight hundred people attend this Spanish-speaking
church every Sunday afternoon. What is unique about this situation is the integration of both congregations. For years the former
Anglo head pastor involved the Latino pastor, Hanibal Rodríguez,
a Colombian, very intentionally in decision-making to such an
extent that, when the Anglo pastor retired, Pastor Hanibal took
over as head pastor of both the Anglo and the Spanish-speaking
congregations. Every Sunday he preaches to both and continues
the practice of interweaving the two congregations and their
church staffs. Latino/a believers of all ages join Anglo volunteers
for CareFest, an annual service day to the broader community; a
growing number participate in summer mission trips. The youth
program combines English and Spanish speakers. Because of this
intermingling, a good number of the Latino/a youth attend the
English Sunday morning service along with some of their parents.

Like other Latino/a congregations, this church supports first-
generation immigrants. There are things this church can offer,
though, that others cannot because of its size and resources. It
provides after-school tutoring and activities in two local elemen-
tary schools and a summer program for older kids from large
nearby apartment complexes, with mostly Latino/a families, that
works on basic academic skills and assists them in finding summer jobs. For adults, the church provides resources to help with

immigration matters and advocacy for public benefits, among other services.

Starting Point Community Church is a small Baptist church located in the Belmont Cragin neighborhood of northwest Chicago, an area that is 80 percent Latino/a. The parents of Pastor Jonathan de la O are from El Salvador. Like many of those who come (attendance is about fifty on Sundays), he is second generation, so the services are bilingual. The denomination has helped with funding and sends inner-city mission groups there to work on the church building, which is quite old.

Pastor Jonathan has a burden for undocumented Latino/a immigrants. To help alleviate the crisis of immigrants staying in police stations and provide a more hospitable environment, this church refurbished part of its education building to house up to twenty immigrant men at a time. Other churches contribute food, and church members and their contacts have donated clothing. The goal is to help these men, who can stay up to two months, transition into society. The church does what it can to help them secure basic legal documents and connect to employment services. The men are encouraged to attend the church services, but, even if they do not, they experience daily the sacrificial grace extended through this amazing pastor and the church members. In addition to taking in these immigrants, Pastor Jonathan and his church distribute care packages to those who remain at the police stations.

Each of these churches, in its own way, is blessing its attendees and its local community. Their vision incorporates care for their own Latino/a people but also embraces the needs in the immediate neighborhood and beyond. Each wrestles with daily life but also reaches out to bless others as they have been blessed by God. *¡Ésta sí es una vida cristiana con propósito!* (This truly is a Christian life with purpose!)

The Old Testament has much to encourage Latinos and Latinas. Through passages like Genesis 12 and Jeremiah 29, it can orient Latino and Latina Christians and churches about how we are to view life as immigrants and as descendants of immigrants. We are changing this country as we bless it in our God's name and with God's help.

5

Equal Participants in the Community of God

New Testament I

Mis abuelos y abuelas, mamá y papá, tíos y tías told me (Miguel) countless stories about how my family left their native Cuba in search of a better life in the US. The vivid nature of their accounts has had a catechizing effect on me in a way that religious instruction would. I'll never forget their words and emotions as they recounted their path to arrive *en los Estados Unidos*. Although they would rather have stayed with their family and friends, they left for a land that provided better opportunities for their family. Years later, *Abuelo Pepe* and *Abuela Fela* would return to the island to see what had become of their loved ones. The hardships they witnessed helped them realize that the decision to move their family had been the right one. Their children and grandchildren would now have opportunities they would never have had in Cuba.

Many Latino/a people have similar stories of how their families left countries like Mexico, Guatemala, and Venezuela in search of a prosperous life in *el Norte*. As we have settled into our new communities, we have realized that some people are not as warm as those in our former countries—not quick to embrace those with strange surnames, especially those without the requisite documentation. In the 1960s, for instance, when my family was in search of housing in Miami, they encountered signs outside of apartment buildings that read, "No Cubans. No children." When they went to the grocery store, some people had the audacity to say, "You are in America. Now speak English!" Everyone in our family can tell stories of locals who felt that it was their duty to make life difficult for those whom they assumed would impoverish their humid corner of Western civilization.

Many Latino/a people who migrate to North America are faithful followers of Jesus Christ. When we arrive in countries like the US and Canada, we expect to feel some relief from *lo cotidiano* in the company of fellow believers. Often enough, our *gente* have experienced a similar marginalization to what we face from the general public, even if expressed more subtly. We have been greeted in churches with phrases like "We don't have a Hispanic ministry," despite that we have yet to open our mouths to say *hola* or *hello*. Even when we join North American churches, expecting to feel the warmth of *familia*, we are often expected to worship in the Spanish-speaking service, despite that many of us are quite fluent in English.

We do not question the decision of many of our *gente* to worship in their native tongue. Spanish, after all, is the language of tens of thousands of churches—many of which have been around for decades and others for over a century. Spanish is also the language of publishing houses that produce valuable resources for millions of people in North America and the language of record companies that produce music for those who sing to their God in *el idioma de los ángeles* (the language of angels). What we do question is why some would assume that we would rather worship with Spanish speakers. Do they suppose *we* would be more comfortable in such a setting? Or would *they* be more comfortable if we worshiped at a safe distance from "the main service"?

Despite our experiences, we concede that there is a path to being considered equal participants in the community of God. But sometimes it comes at a cost—for we must be willing to adopt the cultural distinctives of our North American brothers and sisters. Whether the churches in our host countries are composed of conservatives or liberals, whether they lean Republican or Democrat, almost every group has its own culturally driven expectations for determining who are the "real Christians." Consequently, a Latino/a family will usually be expected to agree with the ecclesial majority's view on any number of social and political issues. Agreement with such extrabiblical "boundary markers"—to borrow a term from Pauline scholarship—may result in being considered an honorary member of God's people. For some, no longer voicing concerns about undocumented immigrants, access to health care for their families, or fair working conditions for migrant workers would be analogous to excising their souls. Others desire to assimilate into their new surroundings, so they store away such concerns in some forgotten corner of their mind. And who could blame them? Latinos and Latinas are used to negotiating for acceptance in their host countries.

But professing Christians do not determine our full inclusion into the people of God. The New Testament supports that we are *fully* accepted into the community of God through the saving work of Jesus Christ—just like anyone else. It even encourages us to resist the pressure to conform to the dominant group's "boundary markers." Our *gente* are undoubtedly included in the one body of Christ, whom the Spirit has empowered for more than just sitting in pews—he has empowered us to be leaders of God's people! We hope this chapter will encourage Latino/a people to live out their full participation in the community of God.

We Are Accepted into God's *Familia*

The Gospel authors lived in the days that prophets like Isaiah and Ezekiel had anticipated for centuries—when God would draw people from all nations into the one *familia* of God. Matthew envisions the fulfillment of such expectations in the arrival of Jesus, the descendant of David and Abraham (Matt. 1:1–6). Matthew's genealogical argument recalls the promise of innumerable descendants to Abraham (Gen. 12, 15, 17) and the promise of a perpetual kingdom to David (2 Sam. 7). Psalm 2 expands the nature of these promises to include all the nations dwelling under the king's rule. Such allusions allow us to envision Jesus as the promised ruler who brings the nations—people from countries like Mexico, Argentina, and Panama—into the people of God. Surely Matthew would have rejoiced to see our *gente* worshiping the promised king.

Matthew reinforces the inclusion of the nations in the family of God with the story of the wise men "from the east" honoring the newborn king (Matt. 2:1–2 NIV). These men are among the first worshipers of King Jesus. This story resonates with many Latin American people today, whose countries celebrate *el Día de Los Reyes* to commemorate the day when Gaspar, Balthasar, and Melchior brought gold, frankincense, and myrrh to the young Christ. *Mi abuela* recalled how children in Cuba would awake to find boxes of hay tucked under their beds, each filled with gifts. When they came to the US, my family—like others from Latin America—neglected to celebrate *el Día de Los Reyes*. But I'm all for recovering the celebration. After all, *el Día de Los Reyes* reminds Latino/a people of how gentiles—those considered outsiders to the covenant promises—were considered worthy of worshiping the Messiah. Just like the wise men, we are *outsiders* who are actually *insiders* in God's kingdom—and we do not come empty-handed. We come from foreign lands with the gifts of our cultures and experiences to enrich Jesus's kingdom. We lay gifts such as bilingualism, multiculturalism, and perseverance through difficult circumstances before King Jesus. We pray that such gifts will edify others and expand Jesus's reign to the ends of the earth.

Mark also assumes the inclusion of the nations into the people of God, claiming that his Gospel is all about "Jesus Christ, the Son of God" (Mark 1:1). The title "Christ" recalls the promise of an anointed Davidic king (2 Sam. 7:8–16). The title "Son of God" recalls Psalm 2, where God promises to grant the son an inheritance of nations (vv. 7–8). Mark applies these titles to Jesus to affirm that he is the promised king who will rule over all the peoples of the earth. Mark then quotes Malachi 3:1 and Isaiah 40:3 to reveal that John is the herald of the new exodus (Mark 1:2–3). Soon, Jesus will gather people from all nations to worship him in a new heaven and new earth, fulfilling the eschatological vision of Isaiah 65–66. Such people will include those who believe that Jesus is the Son of God—like the Roman centurion (Mark 15:39). Although the centurion was a member of Rome's occupying forces, he was also an outsider in the land of Judea—just like many Latinos and Latinas are outsiders in North America. As the Roman centurion's messianic confession testified to his inclusion in the people of God, so also the confessions of millions of Latino/a people in North

America witnesses to their unquestionable acceptance into the believing community.

Luke reinforces the point that the nations are fully accepted members of God's people. He does so by extending Jesus's lineage beyond the Jewish patriarchs David and Abraham, all the way back to Adam and God (Luke 3:23–38). In linking Jesus to the ancestor of all humans (Adam) and the God who made them, Luke shows that God's inclusive grace extends to all humankind, even those to whom some ascribe an inferior status (cf. 10:25–37). Luke's genealogy speaks a powerful word to Latinos and Latinas. Although we sometimes feel like outsiders among the people of God in North America, Luke's words should cause us to embrace our identity as members of *la familia de Dios* (the family of God). We are among the people from all nations whom God is reconciling into one cosmic family.

John's Gospel is even more inclusive than Luke's, providing Latino/a people with even more reason to believe in their equal inclusion into God's family, even in a strange land. In his prologue, he reveals God's intention to redeem the entire creation from darkness and into his restorative light (John 1:1–13; cf. Gen. 1). John confirms the redemptive extent of God's salvation in the account of Jesus's baptism, when the Baptist says, "Look, the Lamb of God, who takes away the sin of the world!" (John 1:29 NIV). When we hear allusions to the exodus from Egypt, we envision that all peoples will take part in the cosmic exodus from the power of sin that once gripped the entire creation.

John includes an account about salvation extending to a Samaritan woman and her community (4:1–45). Their faith in Jesus makes the Samaritans equal members of God's family, despite them being loathed and marginalized among the Israelites. Like the Samaritans, Latino/a people are sometimes from the "wrong part of town."

While there are all kinds of stereotypes associated with *barrios* like Little Havana, East LA, and Union City, we feel at home in neighborhoods where we can find restaurants that serve *arroz con frijoles*, *tacos*, and *platanos maduros*—foods that taste like our *abuela* prepared them. We feel comfortable in spaces where Spanish is common and where people speak English with a Spanish accent. We imagine the Samaritans loved their *barrios* just as much as we love ours. So we resonate with how Jesus revealed himself as the "savior of the world" to the people of Samaria—a place loved by its people but considered to be on the "wrong side of the tracks."

Acts records the Spirit's inclusion of people from Jerusalem (2:1–13), Samaria (8:1–25), and beyond (10:34–48) into the community of God.[1] Throughout the centuries, this community has grown to include people from across the globe—people who speak different languages and come from various cultures. It includes Latinos and Latinas living in countries like the US and Canada. We may prefer the worship music of Richie Rey and Bobby Cruz, and we may be accustomed to living in multigenerational homes with our *abuelos* and *abuelas*. We may even prefer lively preaching that extends well into the lunch hour! Jesus would not expect us to put aside such cultural distinctives when we worship in majority culture contexts. He has already made us equal participants in the community of God. As such, we have the opportunity to enrich the churches in our host countries by bringing our own music, love for *familia*, and even a preference for long sermons!

The lived experiences of Latino/a believers embody the New Testament's vision of the inclusion of outsiders into the people

---

1. The concepts of race and ethnicity in Acts are important for understanding how the Spirit includes diverse peoples into the one community of God. On the use of race and ethnicity in Acts, particularly in Acts 16, see Eric D. Barreto, *Ethnic Negotiations: The Function of Race and Ethnicity in Acts 16*, Wissenschaftliche Untersuchungen zum Neuen Testament 2/294 (Tübingen: Mohr Siebeck, 2010).

of God. But the experiences of Latinos/as can be different from those of majority culture believers, who may have a more difficult time seeing themselves as "outsiders" whom God has graciously drawn into his covenant family. From our perspective, they may unconsciously equate their existence to that of the Jewish people, who were "insiders" to "the divine glory, the covenants, the receiving of the law, the temple worship and the promises" and to whom belong "the patriarchs" and from whom "is traced the human ancestry of the Messiah" (Rom. 9:3–5 NIV). We are not suggesting an ethnic association between first-century Jews and majority culture believers in North America. Our connection is based on the latter's self-perception (often an unconscious one), rather than their ethnic affiliation with Jewish people.

Richard Niebuhr looked back on the history of America and made a similar observation, arguing that nineteenth-century Americans envisioned the kingdom as "destined to bring light to the gentiles by means of lamps manufactured in America."[2] Although we are beyond the period of American industrialization, the spirit of Niebuhr's observation endures: North Americans may understand themselves to have an "insider" status in the people of God, a status analogous to that of Jews in the history of redemption (Rom. 3:1–2; Eph. 2:11–13). They may do so without realizing that the majority of them are beneficiaries of the grace that God has extended to people outside of Jerusalem and Judea. Such readers would do well to consider the interpretations of faithful Latinos/as, which would expand their interpretive horizons and allow them to envision themselves as people from the nations— those who were once "outsiders"—whom God has drawn into his covenant people.

2. H. Richard Niebuhr, *The Kingdom of God in America* (Hamden, CT: Shoestring, 1956), 179.

We Should Resist the Pressure to Conform

The apostle Paul planted and oversaw churches composed of Jews and gentiles. Although the gentiles were the majority in the Pauline communities, Jews were still the original recipients of the covenant promises—as we have argued, they were "insiders." So it was natural for Jews to be the dominant group in some early Christian circles. We see evidence of this in the authority the Jewish pillar apostles—James, Peter, and John—had over the affairs of the earliest Christians (Gal. 2:1–10). Jewish believers who came from James were able to pressure Antiochian believers into observing food laws that discouraged Jews from eating with gentiles (Gal. 2:11–14). We also see the influence of Jews in Galatia, where some sought to compel gentiles to adopt the ethnic distinctives of Judaism (like circumcision, food laws, and Sabbath observance) to be fully accepted into the family of God. If the gentiles refused to adopt such "boundary markers," then they would not be fully accepted into God's family. In his letters, Paul passionately argues against compelling the gentiles to put aside their own ethnic and cultural identities to be considered part of the faithful. They, just like the Jews, have trusted in the same Messiah who brings the nations into one family of God, without conforming to the expectations of the dominant Jewish group (Gal. 2:15–16; 3:7, 14, 22, 26–28). The promises had never been solely for the Jewish people. From the beginning God intended to bless the nations through the descendants of Abraham (Gen. 12:1–3; Isa. 42:6).[3]

Such struggles among the earliest Christian communities are analogous to *la lucha* that Latino/a people often endure in North

3. My reading of the Pauline epistles is influenced by the views of New Perspective proponents such as N. T. Wright and James D. G. Dunn. See Wright's *What Saint Paul Really Said: Was Paul of Tarsus Really the Founder of Christianity?* (Grand Rapids: Eerdmans, 1997), and Dunn's *The New Perspective on Paul* (Grand Rapids: Eerdmans, 2008).

American evangelical contexts. The pressure to conform to the expectations of dominant culture believers can be overwhelming. Latino/a people may even feel like there is no other way to be considered "real Christians."

If Paul were alive to witness the struggles of Latinos and Latinas in their host country churches, he would be astonished that some would even consider adopting the dominant group's identity markers to be considered *real* covenant members. We are not arguing that Latino/a people should resist any semblance of cultural integration. There is always some measure of cultural negotiation necessary to function in a new context, like adjusting oneself to social greetings and new foods. Growing up in Miami, for instance, I would greet every woman with a kiss on the cheek. A kiss had nothing to do with whether I was romantically interested in someone—it was just the way we greeted people of the opposite sex. But when I moved to the Anglo South, I quickly realized that a friendly peck communicated a different cultural message. Yikes! So I opted for a nice "hello" or the occasional high five. I also had to adjust to new foods, like fried okra, green beans loaded with hunks of ham, and white gravy on biscuits. I considered these acceptable, high-caloric substitutes for Cuban food until I could jump on a plane to Miami to get some *croquetas* and *pan cubano*.

Once more, I am *not* arguing that Latinos and Latinas should abstain from all forms of cultural accommodation. I am arguing that we should resist culturally bound expectations of the dominant group, like political and social stances, as well as others, like dress, music, and preaching styles, to be considered legitimate members of the community of God. Such expectations are akin to the "boundary markers" that were imposed on the Galatians. Although our *gente* are not being threatened with the knife of circumcision, the spiritual incisions on our souls are no less painful.

Admittedly, the pressure to conform to the identity markers of the dominant group is relentless, just as it was in Galatia (Gal. 5:1–12; 6:12–16).

In all honesty, I had never experienced the pressure to conform to the majority group's expectations in a Christian church until I left the safe confines of my Protestant church in Miami. In Miami, Cubans and other Latinos/as are the majority, and I was completely ignorant of the broad evangelical culture—something that would quickly change when I moved to the South. Kat Armas's experience sums up my own: "I admit, being raised in an immigrant Roman Catholic community and then transitioning to Protestantism as an adult left me unfamiliar with the ins and outs of evangelicalism. Not only was I blissfully ignorant of what I was stepping into spiritually, but as a Cuban American born and raised in a city predominantly made up of Cuban Americans, I had yet to wrestle with my cultural identity in a majority, non-Hispanic white context."[4]

When I moved to the South, I quickly realized that the worship service really did begin at 10 a.m. sharp. Unlike my home church, the advertised start time was not when we were expected to casually stroll into the sanctuary as the worship team tuned their instruments and the sound team checked the microphones. *Uno, dos, tres.* I also realized that many folks stood for worship the same way they stood in the checkout line at a grocery store—only a little swaying allowed. *¡Rayo!* But I adjusted. I learned to stand in one place and to show up in just enough time to slam the door of my car and sprint to my seat before the congregation sang the first stanza of "Come, Now Is the Time to Worship." I felt like they were playing that song just for me.

4. Kat Armas, *Abuelita Faith: What Women on the Margins Teach Us about Wisdom, Persistence, and Strength* (Grand Rapids: Brazos, 2021), 3.

Yet there are some things I refuse to accept. They still gnaw at me. I find it difficult to believe that I am supposed to love Jesus but show no tangible concern for those crossing the Rio Grande or arriving in Florida on crudely made floats. Churches in Miami are filled with such people! I have seen their love for Jesus! I have also seen how our churches cared for them—the least of these, the very people for whom Jesus died. I also cannot reconcile my love for Jesus with the expectation that faithful Christians would swear allegiance to a political party that favors the rich over the poor, seems to care little for ethnic diversity, and wants to bring back some imagined idyllic period in America. What would James say about favoring the rich? Isn't there going to be a throng of nations worshiping Jesus in the new creation? And when exactly were these ideal days in America? Before the civil rights movement? Was it when Latino/a children in Southwestern states like California and Arizona were not permitted to attend classes with Anglo students?[5] Was it before the days of fair wages for migrant workers?[6] I have never been able to adopt such "boundary markers." To do so would be adopting a gospel that, as Paul argues, is really no "good news" at all—one that binds people to the will of the dominant group rather than to Jesus Christ (Gal. 1:10).[7]

5. Until 1947, for instance, Latino/a children in California were not allowed to attend schools with white children. In *Mendez v. Westminster School District*, however, the court ruled that schools could not separate Latino/a children from white children. This ruling paved the way for the end of segregated schools in California. See Mendez v. Westminster School District, F.2d 774 (9th Cir. 1947).

6. In the 1960s and 70s, César Chávez succeeded at increasing wages and attaining better working conditions for migrants in the Southwestern US. See Matthew García, *From the Jaws of Victory: The Triumph and Tragedy of Cesar Chávez and the Farm Worker Movement* (Berkeley: University of California Press, 2014).

7. For the sake of clarity, I am not supporting one political party over another. I am simply critiquing the way many majority culture Christians would expect allegiance to their preferred political party as a "boundary marker" for being considered a genuine believer.

Latinos and Latinas should not feel compelled to adopt a gospel other than the one Christ preached, which is good news for the captive and sets free the oppressed (Luke 4:18–19; cf. Isa. 61:1–2). In Pauline terminology, we should come to terms with our "righteous" status through faith in Jesus the Messiah (Gal. 2:15–3:14). After all, being "righteous" means that God accepts us as sons and daughters, without us having to conform to any group's ethnic distinctives (Gal. 3:15–4:7; cf. Rom. 4, 8). It also signifies that we have the Spirit, who confirms our inclusion in God's family (Gal. 4:6–7)—the very same Spirit who affirmed the inclusion of Samaritans and gentiles in Acts. Although we may find ourselves in North American churches, where we are considered "one of the faithful" so long as things like our social and political stances line up with those of the majority, the apostle Paul would encourage us to resist such "boundary markers" of inclusion. We are, after all, genuine followers of Jesus Christ, whose political and social concerns are shaped by how the Scriptures speak to our experiences and struggles in our host countries. Paul would strongly encourage our *gente* to live out their status as members of God's family without depending on the acceptance of the dominant group—for we have already trusted in the one who draws the nations into the one people of God and does not privilege the preferences of any ethnic group.

We say all this knowing how the apostle Paul encourages his readers. But we are also Latino/a people, so we understand the pressure to conform to the expectations of the influential. We understand that it can be overwhelming. We even understand that it may cause us to hide our God-given cultural identities as *argentinos/as*, *puertorriqueños/as*, and *colombianos/as*. Who doesn't want to be accepted by their brothers and sisters in Christ? Who doesn't want to be treated "just like everyone else"? But this is where we must listen to Paul, who encourages the Galatians to shun identity markers associated with slavery under the old age (Gal. 4:8–31). The Galatians are free sons and daughters of Abraham, just like Isaac—and so are we! Ultimately, ethnic identity markers, like circumcision or adhering to a set of political and social concerns, mean nothing for our acceptance as God's people (5:6–11). All that matters is the strong faith that our *familias* have exhibited for generations, which results in Spirit-empowered love, joy, peace, patience, kindness, goodness, faithfulness, gentleness, and self-control (5:6, 22–23). This is spiritual fruit that Latinos and Latinas can extend to church members of our host country, without having to conform to their political and social preferences.

Although many dominant culture believers expect Latino/a people to conform to their socially driven expectations, we assume no intended malice—it's just the way their environments have conditioned them to envision faithful believers. Some, however, are more intentional about making "a good showing in the flesh" (Gal. 6:12 NRSV). That is to say, their motivation for pressuring everyone to conform is to show fellow members of the dominant group that they have succeeded in making Latino/a people "just like them." Such enslavement to anyone's expectations cuts against the grain of Paul's liberating gospel.

In reality, no group's boundary-defining distinctives matter in the new creation (Gal. 6:15). All such external requirements are associated with the passing age (6:14). In the new creation, the only fleshly mark that matters is the crucified flesh of Christ—that's what makes Latinos and Latinas equal members of God's family and recipients of the Spirit, who empowers them to be a blessing to the churches in their host countries (6:17). So, Latinos and Latinas can live out a vibrant faith in Christ without having to adopt any group's identity markers. We are recipients of the

Spirit who makes us God's sons and daughters and equal heirs of all God promised his multiethnic people.

We Are One in Christ

Our struggles for equal inclusion in the community of God can leave us angry or bitter. We may even feel like throwing a *chancleta*, also known as a *chancla*, at someone's head. For the uninitiated, a *chancleta* is the Cuban version of a sandal. If I had tested her patience, my Cuban mother would whiz one at me at the speed of light. She rarely missed! When she did, the *chancleta* would usually leave a mark on the wall, which served to deter any future misbehavior. But I understand this may not be the best tactic. Much to the disappointment of *mi mamá*, Paul would encourage us to be long-suffering with Christians who have a difficult time accepting our *gente* into their ecclesial communities. His argument is grounded in the reality that all believers are one in Christ. We have all been redeemed and forgiven of our transgressions through the blood of Jesus Christ (Eph. 1:7). This grace is freely bestowed on all, so that all things in heaven and earth may be united in Christ (1:8–10). The "things on earth" includes all the people whom God created and whom God is now uniting in Christ. All are now one in Christ Jesus and are recipients of the Spirit, who empowers our holiness and assures our status as promised heirs (1:11–14).

We do acknowledge the struggle to live out the unity that Jesus has accomplished through his blood. As much as our *gente* strive for oneness with majority culture believers, many North American churches have difficulty seeing us as those with whom they have been united—that they are equal participants in the same spiritual family as those who come here from countries where Spanish is the primary language. So they keep us at a safe distance—they bring us near but not so near as to sacrifice position and privilege for the sake of unity. Cuban theologian Justo González's diagnosis of American mainline churches may also apply to evangelical contexts:

> A certain instinct tells us that radical evangelism in our society would bring about the conversion, not only of unbelievers, but of the church. And that would be too threatening. Therefore, we make certain that mission flows only in one direction: that the center can affect the periphery, not vice versa. We translate materials into Spanish. We give money to support a Hispanic mission. We appoint a Hispanic pastor to go out there and work among Hispanics. But we are not ready to adjust our structures. . . . We are not ready to share our leadership, to open our cultural paradigms to the give-and-take that true encounter brings about.[8]

That "give-and-take" is expected of those striving for unity. Failure to share power and position results in a tiered ecclesial structure that privileges the dominant ethnic group. This is not the kind of unity for which Jesus died—and it is certainly not what Paul envisioned.

When we are not treated as equals, we must remind ourselves that we are "no longer foreigners and strangers" but "fellow citizens" of God's household, the very temple in which his Spirit dwells (Eph. 2:19; cf. 2:14–22). The interpretive scope of Paul's words certainly includes our *abuelos y abuelos, mamás y papás, hermanos y hermanas, toda nuestra gente latina*. Though we are sometimes kept at arm's length, God has brought us into the same spiritual family as the influential group in our host countries. We should never doubt this reality—for Paul assures us that God has always intended to bring Jews and gentiles (i.e., people from all

8. Justo L. González, *Santa Biblia: The Bible through Hispanic Eyes* (Nashville: Abingdon, 1996), 55.

nations) into one family who will worship the true God without giving superior status to any group (3:1–13).

We Are Examples of Holiness

Since we have been brought into the one family of God, we also have the Spirit, who enables our *gente* to walk "worthy of the Lord . . . bearing fruit in every good work" (Col. 1:10 NIV) and living "holy" lives (1:22). Paul's words should cause us to value *all* whom God has brought into his family, considering them worthy of offering their holy lives in service to our common Lord. Although few would disagree with Paul's argument, the reality is that many majority culture contexts rarely portray ethnic minorities as faithful representatives of God's people. Such spaces usually point to popular majority culture ministers, academics, or denominational figures as examples of holy living.

Latinos and Latinas should not be discouraged by this reality. We should remind ourselves that the apostle Paul considered us worthy recipients of the Spirit, who empowers our faithfulness to Jesus Christ. Besides, we have our own examples of godliness. People like Bishop Óscar Romero, who was murdered for speaking out against the El Salvadorian government's oppression of the poor; Zaida Maldonado Pérez, one of the first Latinas to serve as a professor and dean at an evangelical seminary; and Moisés Silva, a well-known evangelical scholar who has taught at various institutions and published widely in the areas of New Testament and hermeneutics.[9] So many of our *gente* are worthy of our emulation, even those who have not pastored churches or published books.

9. Examples of faithful Latino/a people throughout the centuries abound in Robert Chao Romero, *Brown Church: Five Centuries of Latino/a Social Justice, Theology, and Identity* (Downers Grove, IL: IVP Academic, 2020).

We should not overlook a spiritual bedrock in Latino/a communities—our *abuelitas*. Our *familias* look up to them as examples of persistence, wisdom, and strength.[10] My *abuelitas* were not professional theologians, but they had a steadfast trust in God and were not afraid to threaten me with the dreaded *chancleta*. Through their examples, I learned about faithfulness and perseverance through life's difficulties. Kat Armas identifies her *abuelita* as the Proverbs 31 woman (prodigious, confident, praiseworthy) and relates her example to other Latina women: "The beautiful thing is that my abuelita is one of the millions of abuelitas—as well as the tías (aunts) and madres—who have formed us and our beliefs."[11] We think Paul would agree with our Spanglish: Our *abuelitas*—and our *tías* and *madres*—are examples of holy lives![12]

We Are Leaders

Our *gente* are not just equal participants in the community of God—we are also equally empowered for leadership. Our examples are grounded in the very Scriptures that testify to our full acceptance. The church of Antioch, for instance, recognized people with non-Jewish names like Lucius and Manaen as gifted for leadership (Acts 13:1).[13] Although we may not see many people with surnames like Rodríguez, Vázquez, and Núñez in positions of ecclesial leadership, we have the example of the Antiochenes, whose names

10. I take these qualities from the subtitle of Armas's *Abuelita Faith*.

11. Armas, *Abuelita Faith*, 11.

12. Mujerista theology focuses on the experiences and perspectives of Latinas. See, for instance, Loida I. Martell-Otero, Zaida Maldonado Pérez, and Elizabeth Conde-Frazier, *Latina Evangélicas: A Theological Survey from the Margins* (Eugene, OR: Cascade, 2003).

13. M. Daniel Carroll R., "Latino/a Biblical Interpretation," in *Scripture and Its Interpretation: A Global, Ecumenical Introduction to the Bible*, ed. Michael J. Gorman (Grand Rapids: Baker Academic, 2017), 320.

were just as foreign to first-century Jews as ours are to those in our host countries.

We also have the examples of Timothy and Titus. Timothy was half gentile and half Jew (2 Tim. 1:5).[14] He was *un mestizo*. Many Latino/a people come from "mixed race" backgrounds. Our families may hail from countries like Venezuela and Peru, but our ancestries are often composed of a mixture of people from continents like Asia, Africa, and Europe. We may even have a parent whose family is from South America and one whose family is from North America, whose heritages are tied to ethnic groups that may include Anglo, Black, Asian, and/or European. Our *gente* really are a "mix" of people from all over the globe. That is why Timothy's *mestizo* identity is something many Latino/a people can identify with. Titus's racial makeup may have even been more problematic than Timothy's. As a gentile, he had no Jewish ancestry. That a gentile would have been chosen to lead God's people could have scandalized traditional Jewish believers. Paul could have certainly recognized leaders more acceptable to the dominant Jewish group—people less susceptible to questions about their race. But he doesn't. He recognizes that a *mestizo* and a gentile are called to lead God's people.

The New Testament reveals that Jews like Paul and gentiles like Timothy and Titus are worthy of leading God's people. Individuals from all nations are qualified to lead God's multiethnic people. Although this reality is not always reflected in North American ecclesial contexts, we must not forget that the New Testament does not grant leadership prerogative to any ethnic group. So our *gente* should see biblical characters like Lucius, Manaen, Timothy, and

14. See the helpful commentary of Osvaldo Padilla, *The Pastoral Epistles: An Introduction and* Commentary, Tyndale New Testament Commentaries 14 (Downers Grove, IL: IVP Academic, 2022).

Titus as examples of how God calls us to serve as Christian leaders. Like them, we are also called to minister to God's people. We are not just those who sit in pews. We lead churches! We proclaim Christ! We only need to look in the Scriptures for examples of ethnic minorities deemed worthy to lead God's people.

We Belong

The New Testament supports the full inclusion of Latinos and Latinas in the people of God, without having to adopt any group's ethnic distinctives. We are certainly among those who have trusted in the Messiah, who gave his life to create a unified people. We are also among those indwelled with the Spirit, who empowers us to live holy lives and equips us for service and leadership in God's kingdom. So despite our struggles to be accepted as equal members of God's people in our host countries, authors like Matthew, Luke, and Paul reveal that God is on the side of our *gente*. He supports our inclusion and full participation in the community of God.

The words of New Testament authors should flood our minds when we feel pressure to adopt social and political stances we do not resonate with in order to be accepted into the people of God. Their words should remind us that we do not have to excise our souls, that we do not have to adopt any groups' culturally driven preferences for identifying "real Christians." We *can*, instead, live as those whom Jesus has drawn into his family through his blood. We *can* value and promote our *gente* as examples of holiness, including many of our pastors and scholars and models of everyday faithfulness and perseverance like our *abuelitas*. We *can* also strive to be ecclesial leaders, despite our ethnic minority status in our host countries. We *can* even strive to live out our unity in Christ with those who would rather see us as *outsiders* to the covenant promises. And if we feel the temptation to throw a *chancleta* at someone, we can just remember that Paul calls us to unity, not to leave dents on walls.

The New Testament authors speak words of hope, resistance, and encouragement to those who strive for faithfulness in countries where the people can sometimes be as cold as their climates. Authors like Matthew, Mark, and Paul speak a "better word" than what Latino/a people may be accustomed to experiencing in their host countries. So let's believe their words—for they remind us of how, through Jesus Christ, we are fully accepted into the community of God.

We belong!

6

Diaspora Faith Communities

New Testament II

Jesus has undoubtedly made Latinos and Latinas equal participants in the family of God. So our *gente* should not feel obliged to
conform to any group's socially and politically inclined boundary
markers for inclusion. We should accept our righteous status in
Christ, so we can turn our attention to extending the blessing of
our presence to the people of *el Norte*. We can offer our perseverance *en lo cotadiano*, our quest for racial justice, and fellowship
to those who go out "for the sake of the Name" (3 John 7 NIV).

We offer our presence in contexts as different as our Latino/a
heritages. Many Latinos and Latinas, for instance, worship in
Spanish-speaking communities. These spaces encourage our
people to do more than listen to the preaching or sing along with
the worship songs. We often shout a hearty *¡Amén!* or *¡Aleluya!*
when something in *el idioma de los ángeles* ministers to our souls.

97

Others worship in English-speaking communities, where the majority of attendees are Anglo believers. Though they are comfortable worshiping in English, they may be more acclimated to Latino/a contexts in cities like the Bronx and Chicago, where the preaching is lively and the singing includes the familiar sounds of *bongos* and *guitarras*. Still others gather at multiethnic churches, where people from various backgrounds worship our common Lord.

My experience in North American evangelicalism is tied to predominantly Anglo churches. Of course, it was not always this way. As I shared in the prior chapter, I once worshiped in a predominantly Latino church in Miami. In all honesty, I still feel more comfortable in ecclesial contexts where the worship is in Spanish and the cultures are like my own. This probably has to do with the fact that Spanish was the lingua franca of my home and of the city of Miami at large. No matter where I went—whether doctors' offices, the post office, or department stores—most everyone spoke in Spanish. I did not begin speaking English until my parents put me in grammar school and introduced me to '80s cartoons like *He-Man*—from which I mimicked phrases like "I have the power!" and "By the power of Grayskull!" My entire upbringing, in fact, was in a city where I was surrounded by Cubans and other Latinos/as. So, when I became a Protestant Christian, I naturally chose a congregation filled with Spanish-speaking believers—people more familiar with foods like *yuca* and *frijoles negros* than with meatloaf and mashed potatoes.

Although I deeply love and appreciate the many Anglo brothers and sisters with whom I have worshiped, I still miss spaces populated by Latinos and Latinas. Maybe it's the warmth of our cultures or the familiar music. Maybe it's the *pan con lechón* (roasted pork on Cuban bread) served hot after Sunday service.

Maybe it's the way the conversations flow seamlessly between English and Spanish. Maybe it's the intangibles, like inside jokes or humor grounded in similar backgrounds and experiences. Maybe it's everything! Perhaps I'll experience it again when we are all at home in the new creation.

All in all, my experiences in North American evangelical contexts have left me feeling out of place, like I belong somewhere else. They have served, if you will, to reinforce my "diaspora" status. I use "diaspora" in reference to people being "dispersed in a strange land." The word may be used interchangeably with "exile" and "migrant" and rightly conveys the dispersed existence of Latino/a people in *el Norte*. Latinos and Latinas born in the US and Canada, who more closely identify with people from places like the Dominican Republic and Honduras, may also resonate with the term "diaspora." As we will see throughout this chapter, one of the blessings of being a Latino/a in the strange land of North America is that our contexts have equipped our interpretive horizons to envision *nuestra gente* as members of a holy diaspora in the present age.

As we journey through this chapter, our goal is to encourage our Latino/a people to be blessings in the North American contexts in which we temporarily reside, knowing that God is preparing a better place for us. Whether we worship in English-speaking faith communities or Spanish-speaking ones, whether in predominantly Anglo or Latino/a spaces or in multiethnic ones, we pray that our *gente* take full advantage of their diaspora status.

We Are Diaspora People

The diaspora status of Latino/a people in North America is symptomatic of a greater cosmic reality: all humans are exiles outside of

Eden (Gen. 1–3). Latinos and Latinas are therefore members of a great dispersion of people throughout the fallen age. God's solution to humanity's exile was the covenant with Abraham, which would end the dispersion and bring all nations into a blessed existence in a new Eden (Gen. 12, 15, 17). Israel was supposed to be a kingdom of priests in the land of Canaan, mediating the holiness of God (Exod. 19:6) and drawing the surrounding nations to his "light" (Isa. 49:6). But the Israelites were unsuccessful at their vocation, leading to their exile into nations like Assyria and Babylon (Deut. 28). God, however, did not abandon his plan to rescue his dispersed peoples. Prophets like Isaiah and Ezekiel anticipate that God will return to lead an exodus greater than the one out of Egypt, saving Jews and gentiles out of the fallen age and delivering them into a renewed paradise (Isa. 40–66; Ezek. 36–37).

This narrative backdrop enables us to envision the significance of Matthew 1:1–17, which opens the New Testament with the announcement that Jesus is the descendant of David and Abraham and will lead his people out of exile in Babylon. By the first century, the term "Babylon" had become a significant metaphor for "the powers that oppressed, took captive, and killed the people of God."[1] The mention of Abraham and David is Matthew's way of confirming that Jesus is the promised royal offspring who will reign over the people of the earth (Gen. 12, 15; 2 Sam. 7; Ps. 2). He will lead his followers on a new exodus out of exile in the present age and deliver them into a new Eden that will extend to the ends of the earth (cf. Gen. 1:28).

Presently, God is still leading his people through the fallen age until we enter the redeemed creation (Rom. 8:12–15). That means

1. Scot McKnight with Cody Matchett, *Revelation for the Rest of Us: A Prophetic Call to Follow Jesus as a Dissident Disciple* (Grand Rapids: Zondervan Reflective, 2023), 47. See 4 Ezra 15:46–47 and 2 Baruch 11:1–3.

we are still dispersed outside of Eden. Peter recognizes this reality, calling his readers "God's elect, exiles" who are dispersed[2] in places like "Pontus, Galatia, Cappadocia, Asia and Bithynia" and who await their "inheritance that can never perish, spoil or fade" (1 Pet. 1:1, 4 NIV). Their dispersion into such places is symptomatic of living in Babylon (5:13). Babylon, of course, is a metaphor for living in an age characterized by empires that oppress God's people. For Peter's readers, their direct oppressor was Rome, which did not take kindly to those who refused to participate in its idolatries and vices.[3] Consequently, faithful slaves and wives could expect physical punishment and even sexual abuse at the hands of their masters and husbands, respectively (2:18–20; 3:1–6). On the whole, believers could expect to be mistreated for their allegiance to the Lord Jesus Christ (4:1–4).[4]

Similarly, James addresses his audience as the "twelve tribes" of the dispersion (1:1).[5] While some take "twelve tribes" as a reference to ethnic Israel, it is more likely that the phrase refers to spiritual Israel in the present world awaiting the inheritance of the coming one (James 2:5).[6] Drawing a connection between his readers and

2. The NIV renders διασπορά as "scattered." We understand the term, in keeping with its common use in Old Testament and Second Temple literature and in the context of 1 Peter, as "a state or condition of being scattered, *dispersion*" (Walter Bauer, Frederick William Danker, William F. Arndt, and F. Wilbur Gingrich, *Greek-English Lexicon of the New Testament and Other Early Christian Literature*, 3rd ed. [Chicago: University of Chicago Press, 2000], 236). See Isa. 49:6 and 2 Macc. 1:27.

3. J. Ramsey Michaels, *1 Peter*, Word Biblical Commentary 49 (Nashville: Thomas Nelson, 1988), 53; Thomas R. Schreiner, *1 & 2 Peter and Jude*, Christian Standard Commentary 37 (Nashville: Holman Reference, 2020), 21.

4. Schreiner, *1 & 2 Peter and Jude*, 21.

5. As in 1 Pet. 1:1, διασπορά should be rendered as "dispersed" or "dispersion."

6. We are not denying the trials of Jews in the first century. Antisemitism was as real then as it is today. James is using "twelve tribes" in a more idealized, eschatological sense, which incorporates Jews and gentiles into the spiritual people of God dispersed in the present age. This sense is consistent with passages such as 1 Pet. 1:17; 2:11; Heb. 11:8–16; and 13:14.

the saints before them, the author of Hebrews argues that old covenant believers were strangers and exiles on the earth who were seeking a better homeland (Heb. 11:13–16). Such texts affirm the present status of believers as exiles dispersed in strange lands—a people susceptible to the trials of living in an age that opposes and oppresses those devoted to the true Lord of the earth.

For many Latinos and Latinas, dispersion is not an abstract theological concept—it is an unavoidable reality. Some have fled oppressive governments in Cuba and Venezuela and arrived in places like Orlando, Jersey City, and Boston. The experience of our *gente* is not unlike the experience of the holy family, who fled Egypt to escape Herod's persecution (Matt. 2). Others have fled drug cartel wars in countries like Colombia and Mexico. Still others have simply come for better job prospects and opportunities for their families, perhaps even to chase the American dream. Although our reasons are varied, Latinos/as would likely agree that we hope our sojourn to *el Norte* will result in better lives for our loved ones. That's why so many are willing to endure the struggles of relocation, which include finding new faith communities, acquiring a suitable home and reliable transportation, and obtaining gainful employment.

But once we establish ourselves, we are not content with just getting by—we want to thrive! We want to be successful! And we want the same for our children and grandchildren! Latinos and Latinas are known for their entrepreneurial spirit. Statistics show that nearly one in four new businesses are owned by Latinos/as and nearly five million of our businesses contribute over eight hundred billion dollars to the US economy![7] *¡Qué logros!* (What an accomplishment!)

7. "Hispanic Entrepreneurs and Businesses Are Helping to Drive the Economy's Entrepreneurial Growth and Job Creation," Joint Economic Committee,

Despite our accomplishments, we are cognizant of our diaspora status in North America. We understand that we may have to work harder than the average native-born citizen to achieve things like job promotions and buying a home. We understand that we may be stereotyped as "hard workers"—which we take as a compliment, so long as it does not associate us only with manual labor. There is nothing wrong with choosing a vocation such as construction or farming. These are honest professions that provide an adequate standard of living for many families. What we reject is being stereotyped as those who work "hard" at mainly one kind of job. The reality is that Latinos/as are lawyers, politicians, professors, and CEOs. We are clergy, dentists, and medical doctors. We are surgeons, engineers, grammar school teachers, and so much more!

Even the fact that we must justify our presence in other labor fields makes us cognizant of our diaspora status in *el Norte*. There are also the occasional—sometimes too occasional—rude comments and unfriendly interactions, which make our outsider status hard to ignore. But what are our options? Go back to communist governments? Go back to places that threaten our family's livelihood? No chance. So we persevere and strive to excel, despite the difficulties of life in cities like Toronto, Nashville, Dallas, Portland, and Vancouver.

Although there are very real struggles associated with diaspora life, we want to return to what we said earlier—that diaspora life can be a blessing. After all, our lives as outsiders in *el Norte* enable us to envision our identity as exiles in the present world, anticipating the inheritance of a place where we will be home with a

---

November 4, 2021, https://www.jec.senate.gov/public/index.cfm/democrats/2021
/11/hispanic-entrepreneurs-and-businesses-are-helping-to-drive-the-economy-s
-entrepreneurial-growth-and-job-creation.

Messiah who will reign over us in peace and prosperity forever. So we identify with Peter's and James's readers (1 Pet. 1:1; James 1:1) and even with old covenant saints like Abraham and Moses (Heb. 11), who recognized their diaspora status in the present world and expected the reward of a better homeland (11:14).

We Are Members of a Holy Diaspora

The same New Testament authors who speak to our diaspora status also speak to how we should live out our days in exile. The author of Hebrews, for instance, spends the first ten chapters of his letter encouraging readers to follow Jesus into their eschatological inheritance. To draw continuity between his readers and the saints before them, he argues that old covenant saints like David, Samuel, and the prophets understood that they were strangers on the present earth and were willing to undergo various sufferings because they anticipated the inheritance of a better place (Heb. 11:1–40). The author of Hebrews encourages readers to consider the saints who preceded them as they "run with perseverance" through the present life to enter Jesus's unshakable kingdom (12:1 NIV; cf. 12:18–29). Their life should be marked by holiness—a life characterized by hospitality and avoiding vices such as sexual immorality—as they await the realization of their lasting city (13:1–19).

Peter acknowledges that his readers have undergone trials, marginalization, and slander at the hands of those who have viewed them with suspicion and hostility (1 Pet. 1:6; 2:12; 4:4).[8] He advises them to live out their exile in holiness (1:17). They should live as those redeemed from their sinful ways through the shed blood of

8. Schreiner, *1 & 2 Peter and Jude*, 131.

God's lamb, Jesus Christ (1:18–19). Peter characterizes holy living as loving one another (1:22); putting aside all malice, deceit, and envy (2:1); offering our lives as spiritual sacrifices to God (2:5); and proclaiming the excellencies of the God who has called his people out of darkness and into his marvelous light (2:9). He also characterizes holy living as being united to one another, sympathetic, and having a tender heart and a humble disposition (3:8). He even calls readers to obey civil authorities, to live out domestic relationships in submission to Jesus Christ, and to pursue peace (2:13–3:11; cf. Ps. 34:12–16). In short, Peter expects that his dispersed readers will live holy lives in the face of a suspicious and hostile culture.

Latino/a believers in North America sometimes face a similar distrust and animosity in North America. Our "strangeness" is only accentuated by the fact that we tend to preserve unique cultural distinctives. One such distinctive is the *quinceañera* celebration, which marks a girl's entrance into womanhood. Although it is often compared to a sweet sixteen celebration, the pomp of *quinceañera* is more like an elaborate wedding. Parents often save for their entire lives—some even go into debt—to throw a party complete with choreographed dancing, an elegant meal, and plenty of refreshments. And then there is the dress: the *quinceañera* usually wears a dress fit for a queen. In Miami, the celebration was so common that I would routinely see fifteen-year-old girls dressed like Queen Isabella posing for pictures in parks, on the beach, or in front of an ornate fountain. Although I am now a long way from the *quinceañera* paradise of Miami, on occasion I arrive at my seminary campus and see a young Latina wearing an ornate dress and posing for pictures near one of our large magnolia trees. *Mamá* and *abuela*, of course, are standing nearby to approve of the pictures and to make helpful (and mildly threatening) suggestions.

¡Sonríe! ¡Enderézate! (Smile! Stand up straight!). Their commands can be so direct that I sometimes find myself involuntarily smiling and standing straight! *Mamá* and *abuela* are also around to threaten anyone who gets within fifty feet of the staging area. I don't know of anyone who has ever penetrated their perimeter and made it out alive. *Dios sabe.* They also play an important role at the celebration, ensuring that everyone behaves and that everything goes according to plan. Anyone who tests their patience should remember that a *tacón*—a high-heeled shoe capable of reaching supersonic speeds—is well within reach.

The perseveration of the *quinceañera* celebration is just one example of how Latinos and Latinas value cultural traditions. We also value multigenerational homes, preserving the Spanish language, foods associated with our family's country (or countries) of origin, and so much more. We do want to fit in to our North American contexts—but not at the expense of losing our cultural identities. We understand that this may mean that members of our host countries consider us "strange," which may result in a similar kind of ostracization and slander to what Peter's readers encountered.

When our experiences reinforce our status as exiles in our present lands, we must listen to biblical authors like James, who exhorted his dispersed readers to regard their trials as tests of their faith, which will lead to their maturity (James 1:2–4). If we lack wisdom in how to live out the time of our dispersion, we should consider how James encourages his audience to confidently petition God (1:5–8). They will receive wisdom in matters such as being slow to anger (1:19–20), taming the tongue (1:26–27; 3:1–12), avoiding partiality toward the rich (2:1–13), not boasting about tomorrow (4:13–17), and being patient in suffering until the return of the Lord Jesus (5:7–11). We should be encouraged to know that the one who perseveres will receive "the crown of life" when Jesus returns to restore his people into the promised kingdom (1:12; cf. 2:5).

Although John does not use explicitly exilic language, his advice is also applicable to Latino/a people—for he reminds us that we are of the "light" and not of the "darkness." The light is symbolic of eternal life associated with the new age (John 1:4–9; 1 John 1:5–7). The darkness is symbolic of the passing age associated with the fallen creation (John 1:4–5; 1 John 1:5–7). As we are exiled in the present age, John expects that we will love God and others—what has always been expected of God's people (1 John 2:7–14; 3:11–24; 4:7–21; 2 John 2–6; cf. Exod. 20). This means, among other things, avoiding those who claim that Jesus did not really come in the flesh (1 John 4:1–6; 2 John 7–10), abstaining from hating others (1 John 3:11–15), and showing hospitality to strangers (3 John 5–8). Living faithfully in the present age reveals that we belong to God (1 John 2:14; 3:19–24; 4:7–21). Our perseverance in holiness will result in being made like Jesus, the very one who exemplified love for God and neighbor by giving his life for humanity (3:1–3, 16).

The advice of authors like Peter, James, and John enables Latino/a people to develop a redemptive perspective on our difficulties in *el Norte*. Our holiness through suffering is in obedience to the God who has "called [us] out of darkness" and "into his marvelous light" (1 Pet. 2:9 NRSV). God has sent his indwelling Spirit to empower all his people to live holy lives (Acts 2:1–13; 8:14–17; 10:41–48; cf. Ezek. 36:25–27). Latino/a believers are most certainly among those whom the Spirit empowers to live holy lives in the places into which we have been dispersed, awaiting the day when we are resurrected to dwell in the cosmic kingdom.

Justo González argues that we are called to live in light of *mañana*. "True, *mañana* is not yet today, but today can be lived out of the glory and promise of *mañana*, thanks to the power of the Spirit."[9] By the power and presence of the Spirit, we can live now as citizens of the coming city, as subjects of the one whose reign will have no end. But our witness to the good news is credible only insofar as we too live as those who believe the message and are willing to stake our lives on it. To love our neighbor, to do justice, to announce peace, to care for the widow and orphan—all these are not things we do beyond or apart from proclaiming the good news.[10] González rightly highlights the holiness our *gente* can exhibit in anticipation of God's consummated reign on the earth. That we can live in light of *mañana*!

We Are Witnesses to Believers and Unbelievers

Latinos and Latinas should envision that God has a redemptive purpose for our holy lives: to open the eyes of unbelievers to their enslavement to the powers of sin and death. Additionally, we should envision that God can use our witness to enlighten fellow Christians to their identity as diaspora people. We should not be surprised, however, when followers of Christ reject our witness to the common identity we share as exiles in the present age. When we encounter such trials, we should remember the words of Jesus: "In this world you will have trouble. But take heart! I have overcome the world" (John 16:33 NIV). The one whose death and resurrection resulted in his victory over the present world has already sent his Spirit to empower our witness through our present struggles (John 14–16). We should therefore rely on the Spirit's enablement to be holy witnesses to unbelievers and believers.

9. Justo L. González, *Mañana: Christian Theology from a Hispanic Perspective* (Nashville: Abingdon, 1990), 164.
10. González, *Mañana*, 167.

Our Witness to Unbelievers

The apostle Peter recognizes the importance of his readers' witness to unbelievers in Asia Minor. He even understands that their status as "dispersed" or "exiled" believers has resulted in various sufferings (1 Pet. 1:2; 2:12; 3:9; 4:12–19; 5:9). He wants them to understand, however, that their difficulties are not unique—it's the reality of believers "throughout the world" (5:9 NIV). More importantly, it was also the reality of Jesus Christ, who suffered unjustly (2:21–25). Peter draws on suffering servant imagery from Isaiah 52–53 to stress that believers are called to endure difficulties, just like their Messiah (1 Pet. 2:21). Though his readers' suffering does not have propitiatory significance, they are called to endurance through hardship and persecution so that the "light" of salvation might extend to places like Pontus, Galatia, Cappadocia, and Bithynia (1 Pet. 2:21; cf. Isa. 49:6).

As Latinos and Latinas, we should envision that God can use our witness to extend the "light" of salvation into places like New Orleans, Vancouver, and San Francisco. Although we will likely endure sufferings of various kinds, we must remember that Jesus endured the shame of a cross for the redemption of humanity. As we live honorably during the time of our dispersion in *el Norte*, unbelievers may envision the character of the holy God whom they may worship on the day of his return (1 Pet. 2:12).

We understand that readers may question our advice. Some may ask, Would it not be preferable to shelter ourselves in the safe spaces of our Latino/a faith communities? For the sake of our sanity and well-being, would it not be better to restrict our contact to those who understand our struggles? Why subject ourselves to any more stereotypes and racist attitudes? We empathize with these questions. We would say that, in some cases, a person who has endured prejudice and bigotry may want to retreat for a time to the confines of Latino/a faith communities who are equipped to minister to their unique struggles. We even understand that some may choose to retreat altogether from difficult ecclesial and institutional spaces that dismiss their struggles, as if trials were figments of our imagination. Racism and marginalization certainly take spiritual and physical tolls, so it makes sense that some people would need to retreat from unhealthy environments.

Whether we remain in difficult spaces or choose to leave them, the harsh reality is that sin is a cosmic force that envelops the entire present age (Rom. 5:21). We simply cannot avoid all difficult circumstances. At one time or another, we will encounter the pain and suffering of living in the present world. And when we do, we should remind ourselves of Peter's words—that God can use our lives to draw unbelievers to worship the one who suffered for their transgressions.

Once again, however, we understand the struggles of dispersion in the present age. We also understand that the pain may be especially acute for Latino/a people, who can be seen as outsiders in North America at large and in the very evangelical spaces where we would expect to feel the acceptance of *familia*. As we wrestle with the role of suffering in our lives, we should remind ourselves that even the apostles misunderstood that they were to follow in the suffering ways of their Messiah (Mark 8–10). Peter even rejected the place of suffering in Jesus's life: "Never, Lord! . . . This shall never happen to you!" (Matt. 16:22 NIV). So Jesus rebukes him, for he knows that there is no redemption without a suffering Messiah (16:23). After Jesus's resurrection, Peter comprehends the role of suffering in the life of Jesus and his followers, so much so that he tells the recipients of his first letter that it is "to this [they] were called" (1 Pet. 2:21 NIV).

Centuries removed from Peter's first letter to the saints in Asia Minor, Jesus's followers are still called to accept the redemptive purpose of their suffering in the present age. God may be so kind as to use the trials of our North American Latino/a faith communities to bear witness to Jesus's propitiatory sacrifice. Suffering, then, may be our greatest witness to the good news of Jesus Christ. Samuel Escobar puts it well:

> Jesus' crucifixion is also the mark of a lifestyle to which the followers of Jesus are called and which also characterizes the Christian missionary style. . . . If we are followers of the Christ who died on the cross, we will undertake missionary work in a way that is consonant with Jesus' own missionary style. This is a style devoid of triumphalism, of manipulative intentions, of reliance on military, economic, technological, or social power. It is a style that draws on all the resources and gifts that God provides and that knows how to read the signs of the times, but that most of all is marked by the spirit of service that characterized Jesus himself.[11]

Escobar's comments crystallize the missionary calling of Latino/a believers in North America. We live holy lives amid sufferings, just like Jesus did, in the hopes that those who were once hostile to us will become members of the same spiritual family.

As we emphasize the place of suffering, we must also realize that we are still living in an age that has not fully given way to the coming one. We are living, if you will, in a dialectic tension between the new age that has "already" arrived and the new one that has "not yet" been fully consummated. Our existence "between the times" should cause us to inhabit a place of Spirit-empowered advocacy

---

11. Samuel Escobar, *In Search of Christ in Latin America: From Colonial Image to Liberating Savior* (Downers Grove, IL: InterVarsity, 2019), 327.

for those suffering in a world where sin still exercises its oppressive grip. Such activism is firmly grounded in our faithfulness to the Lord who gave his life to deliver the entire creation from the painful effects of sin (John 3:16). Latinos and Latinas have a long history of such Spirit-led and faith-grounded advocacy. Robert Chao Romero highlights the witness of Latino/a people, showing how they have promoted a Jesus who came to "save, redeem, and transform every aspect of our lives and the world."[12] More specifically, Jesus's "salvation extends over all God's creation, which has become twisted and corrupted as a consequence of sin. This includes everything distorted in our world—whether personal, familial, social, or global. Nothing is left out. It includes our personal emotional brokenness and dysfunctional family relationships, but also, poverty, racism, slavery, human trafficking, oppression of immigrants, warfare, lack of clean water, AIDS, gang violence, and lack of educational opportunity."[13]

Latinos and Latinas like archbishop Óscar Romero, Elizabeth Conde-Frazier, and C. René Padilla are examples of those who have promoted the holistic good news of Jesus Christ.[14] Upon the bedrock of this message, and the generations of those who have gone before us, Latino/a people can advocate for social change in anticipation of the full realization of a redeemed cosmos that we do "not yet" see (Rom. 8:25). We do this through our advocacy for just immigration laws; our push for educational, employment, and housing equity for our *gente* and other disadvantaged groups; and so much more. We do so knowing that our Spirit-driven activism and the results thereof can give unbelievers a vision of the

12. Robert Chao Romero, *Brown Church: Five Centuries of Latina/o Social Justice, Theology, and Identity* (Downers Grove, IL: IVP Academic, 2020), 12.

13. Chao Romero, *Brown Church*, 12.

14. C. René Padilla, *Mission between the Times: Essays on the Kingdom* (Grand Rapids: Eerdmans, 1985).

human flourishing they can experience under the cosmic reign of Jesus.

Maybe it's in our advocacy, as we are enabled by the Spirit to roll back the forces of darkness, that we will face our fiercest trials. As we encounter such difficulties, we should remind ourselves that our suffering can bear witness to the Messiah who gave his life to deliver the entire created order out of the "present evil age" dominated by sin and death (Gal. 1:4). *¡Somos testigos de las buenas nuevas!* (We are witnesses of the good news!)

Our Witnesses to Believers

The holy witness of our *gente* is also beneficial for those who have a difficult time envisioning themselves as strangers on the present earth. In chapter 5, we argued that some majority culture believers may struggle to understand their exilic status. It may be that their allegiance is tied more closely to nations like the US than to an imperishable cosmic kingdom for all who worship a once-crucified-now-resurrected Messiah. Latino/a believers should embrace the opportunity to live out their diaspora status before such members of God's *familia*. God can use our witness to strengthen the faithfulness of those whose allegiance may be too closely aligned to a kingdom that is already in the process of passing way.[15]

We believe our advice is grounded in the writings of New Testament authors like Paul, who envisions that believers can be of great encouragement to one another. He argues, for instance, that the faithfulness of Roman churches is an inspiration to believers throughout the world (Rom. 1:8; 16:19). He hopes to visit the Romans so that they can be mutually encouraged by each other's

---

15. I draw this insight from M. Daniel Carroll R., "Latino/a Biblical Interpretation," in *Scripture and Its Interpretation: A Global, Ecumenical Introduction to the Bible*, ed. Michael J. Gorman (Grand Rapids: Baker Academic, 2017), 321.

faithfulness (1:12; 8:12–25). Paul also boasts about the Thessalonians' exemplary faithfulness and perseverance amid persecutions and sufferings as they await the return of Jesus Christ (1 Thess. 2:3–4). As with the Romans, Paul believes that the Thessalonians' faithful example is beneficial for the churches of Christ (2 Thess. 1:4). Paul points to other examples of faithfulness, such as the household of Stephanus (1 Cor. 16:15), the Philippians (Phil. 1:3–11), Epaphras (Col. 4:12–13), Timothy (1 Tim. 1:2; 2 Tim. 1:3–7), and Titus (Titus 1:4), whose devotion is an encouragement to other believers.

Peter and John provide their readers with similar advice. Peter contends that believers should find solace in the fact that their brothers and sisters are enduring similar sufferings, which will one day result in their restoration, confirmation, strengthening, and establishment into an imperishable inheritance (1 Pet. 5:9–10; cf. 1:3–9). In his epistles, John finds comfort in the example of those who are living faithfully as they await the light of the new creation to overcome the present age of darkness (e.g., 1 John 1:5–10; 4:7–21; 2 John 4; 3 John 5–7). Later in Revelation, John encourages believers to look at the example of churches in Smyrna (Rev. 2:8–11) and Philadelphia (3:7–13), who were called to persevere in faithfulness so that they might overcome life in the present age and enter the new creation promised to God's people (Rev. 20–22).

These are important examples of biblical authors who find comfort in the faithfulness of other believers and who encourage their readers to do the same. But what if believers do not notice our holy lives? Should we draw attention to our Latino/a people? We should first consider our motivation. Are we boasting about ourselves for our own benefit? If anyone had reason to boast, it was certainly Paul—but even he says that he boasts only in the cross of Christ (Gal. 6:14). In the context of Galatians, Paul refuses to boast in boundary markers like circumcision for being considered a genuine member of God's people (6:15). It has nothing to do with drawing attention to his life for the sake of strengthening other believers. In 2 Corinthians, he urges readers to look at the example of his suffering and that of his fellow workers to encourage them amid their own afflictions (2 Cor. 1:3–11). Paul also encourages the Philippians to know that his sufferings have served to advance the gospel and to increase believers' confidence in the Lord (Phil. 1:12–14).

Such examples show how Latinos and Latinas can also draw attention to our *gente* for the edification of fellow believers in North America. Our faith communities can be like the churches in Rome, Thessalonica, and Philadelphia, whose faithfulness amid suffering testified to their status as people dispersed in the present age. We can draw attention to our Latino/a faith communities through teaching, preaching, and writing books. We can also be tireless advocates for Latinos/as in institutional and ecclesial meetings and conversations. There are all kinds of ways that we can draw attention to the holy lives of Latinos and Latinas for the benefit of the body of Christ. Drawing attention to their faithfulness will hopefully give believers a glimpse of our shared identity as exiles dispersed in the present age, a people whose citizenship is tied to a kingdom that Jesus will establish on the earth.

If our encouragement is met with resistance, we must keep exhorting believers to look to the holy example of our *gente*. It may be that they lack what Willie James Jennings calls the "Christian imaginary" necessary to move away from envisioning themselves as the rightful owners of their present lands to those who are dispersed in the fallen age.[16] When believers move away from envisioning their

16. I draw the language of "social imaginary" from Willie James Jennings without claiming that he makes the same argument about Christians dispersed

present North American contexts as divinely granted to them by God, which only creates a sense of "national insularity," we may begin to count ourselves among the many people whom God has destined for community on a new earth (Ps. 60; 61; 72).[17] Latinos and Latinas therefore have an important role to play in the lives of North American believers to expand their imaginations to envision themselves as exiles on the present earth.

We are uniquely equipped for such a task because our existence in places like Raleigh, Phoenix, and Austin—where we are not quite at home but also not able to return to our countries of origin—reinforces our status as exiles on the present earth. Our "existential experience" therefore creates a strong sense of homelessness,[18] which is a feeling unknown to many Christians in *el Norte*. Even Latino/a people born in the US and Canada grow up hearing stories of their family's life in countries like Cuba and Guatemala, which make their hearts long for places they have never visited. We suspect that what they long for is the place where all humanity will be home with their God; the place Isaiah and John describe as a new heaven and a new earth, otherwise known as a new Eden (Isa. 65–66; Rev. 21–22). This is the Edenic existence for which we can encourage our brothers and sisters in Christ to long—when we live out our status as holy exiles in the present age, a people whose allegiance is more closely tied to the kingdom in the coming world than to any present nation. The entire world, after all, belongs to the God who is making it into a place fit for all God's people.

---

in the present age. See Jennings, *The Christian Imagination: Theology and the Origins of Race* (New Haven: Yale University Press, 2010).

17. I am again drawing from Jennings without claiming that we are arriving at the same conclusions. Jennings, *Christian Imagination*, 215.

18. See Justo L. González, *Santa Biblia: The Bible through Hispanic Eyes* (Nashville: Abingdon, 1996), 103–13.

All this shows how Latino/a diaspora faith communities can be blessings to their host countries! God may certainly use the holy witness of Latinos and Latinas to draw unbelievers into our spiritual *familia*. He can also use our witness to expand the "Christian imaginary" of believers to envision themselves as members of God's dispersed people throughout the present age, awaiting the inheritance of their eschatological home. *¡Podemos ser una bendición a nuestras comunidades y la sociedad en general en Norte América!* (We can be a blessing to our communities and North American society in general!)

CONCLUSION

The six chapters of this book cover a lot of ground. This is a work that is primarily inward facing—that is, we attempt to speak words of encouragement to our *pueblo* (Latino and Latina believers) and to our churches that are grounded in the Bible, both Old and New Testaments. At the same time, we invite others to accompany us in our readings to discover new things in Scripture or to come to value well-known texts in a fresh way.

Two interlocking themes emerge across these pages that are foundational for Latino and Latina Christian communities in the US today. The first are matters related to *identity*. On the one hand, there is how we, as Latinos and Latinas, perceive ourselves. Here, both our cultural backgrounds (customs, language, food, family, music, and more), so worthy of celebration, and the legal status of many of us come into play. These are complex, in-house, ongoing discussions. Inescapably, they must be processed and negotiated within the broader arena of the majority culture and society in which Latinos and Latinas are often perceived as a minority of outsiders, of *intrusos* (intruders) in a world different from their own.

A second concern, which builds on the first, is how to live as faithful Christians in such circumstances. Latinos and Latinas sometimes groan under the weight of our burdens. Does our God hear our groaning? How should Latino and Latina believers handle our challenges and disappointments? And as we lift our eyes to the horizon, can we envision the Latino/a church contributing to the national church and even, more widely, to the country at large?

It is here that we turn to the Bible. In doing so, we can begin to appreciate the important elements that Latinos and Latinas can bring to our readings of the Scripture. This is the topic of the first chapter. There we see that our church communities embrace the Bible as the very Word of God, trusting in its truth and power. We read it from our particular location as a largely immigrant community or as descendants of immigrants from every country in Latin America, who turn to the Lord for guidance and encouragement. Chapter 2 explains that Latinas and Latinos encounter this Word straightforwardly (*sencillamente*), not only as individuals and families but also as churches and as part of the Latino/a diaspora (*en conjunto*), in our journeys of life in this country (*en el camino*).

The next four chapters explore these two issues of identity and direction through the study of the Bible, with two chapters probing each testament. Chapter 3 presents several Old Testament stories about God's people migrating and their lives in foreign lands, much of which resonates with Latino and Latina believers in the US today. We see trials and tribulations of all kinds, as well as pilgrimages of faith in God. Chapter 4 directs our attention to the call of God's people to be a blessing, even when we are a minority in a foreign setting. This charge can help Latino and Latina believers and churches to reframe our self-understandings and recognize that we are protagonists in the Lord's mission in the world. In the Old Testament, we learn that followers of God are significant because of who we are and what we can be for ourselves and for others. The identity question has broadened.

The New Testament chapters extend the themes of identity and purpose. We learn in chapter 5 that these themes are enriched by new realities brought with the coming of Jesus and the establishment of the church. There is no need to forsake our Latino/a identities and conform to the culture of the majority church. We are included in God's family through the same gospel and Spirit and, as Latinos and Latinas, are empowered to participate in and lead God's people. All Christians are sojourners in this world, as chapter 6 makes clear, but the Latino/a community's realities are more than spiritual; its diaspora is a lived reality. In this time before the consummation of all things, in anticipation of *mañana*, the diaspora Latino/a church can be a fruitful witness and a blessing to unbelievers and fellow Christians alike.

In sum, Latinos and Latinas come to the Scriptures with a deep, sincere trust that is rewarded. In the Bible we see ourselves, individually and as a people, in the lives of those in its pages. Those ancients trusted God and enjoyed faithful divine care in their day-to-day challenges, even as they saw that their presence mattered to the Lord and to the nations. And this is how we too are to live. With full confidence in God's guidance and care, as Christian Latinos and Latinas we can embrace our cultural and spiritual identities and fulfill our calling to be light in a world that sometimes does not understand or even accept us. At the same time, we know that these commitments and insights contribute to biblical, theological, and missiological reflection for the broader church. What we believe and proclaim about God, the life of faith, and the human condition is beneficial and urgent for all Christians.

The Bible tells us so. *Bendito sea el Señor* (blessed be the Lord).

NAME INDEX

SCRIPTURE INDEX

TOPIC INDEX